THE NAMING OF AMERICA

Also by Allan Wolk
The Presidency and Black Civil Rights:
Eisenhower to Nixon

THE NAMING OF AMERICA

OF

AMERICA

☞ HOW CONTINENTS, COUNTRIES, ☞ STATES, COUNTIES, CITIES, TOWNS, ☞ VILLAGES, HAMLETS, & POST OFFICES CAME BY THEIR NAMES ☞

BY ALLAN WOLK

THOMAS NELSON INC., PUBLISHERS
Nashville / New York

First edition

Library of Congress Cataloging in Publication Data

Wolk, Allan.
  The naming of America.

  Includes index.
  1. Names, Geographical—United States.   2. United States—History, Local.   I. Title.
E155.W64   973   77-31833
ISBN 0-8407-6562-2

Acknowledgments

This book could not have been compiled without the enthusiastic assistance I received from hundreds of Americans throughout the nation—postmasters, local residents, town historians, historical societies, etymologists, librarians, assistants to governors and mayors, and chambers-of-commerce members. Everyone listed below has played a part in this book:

Nancy C. Adams, George B. Abdill (director, Douglas County Museum, Oregon), Ida C. Abshire, Joy Alleman, Jewill R. Alverson, Yosh Amano, Charles S. Anderson, Raymond G. Antoine, Mayor William C. Armagasti (Hooversville, Pennsylvania), Helen W. Armstrong, Mayor Byron Baker (Weeping Water, Nebraska), Edith Ballow, G. C. Barfield, L. W. Barnes, Dudley Bayne (city manager, Hereford, Texas), James C. Beardsley, S. Bell, Leopold E. Benjamin, Governor Robert F. Bennett (Kansas), Lilafinn Bessire (Grant County Historical Society, Kansas), Margaret Bettschen, Ernest Bickhaus, Evelyn Bird, Eliza Bishop, John B. Black, Louis G. Black, Arnold A. Blackmur, Mrs. Elvin Block, Mrs. L. M. Bolton, Governor David L. Boren (Oklahoma), Robert G. Bradshaw (Carroll County Historical Society), Helen Bratton, Velma R. Bray, A. Gordon Brooks, Arnett Brown, Governor Dolph Briscoe (Texas), J. C. Bryant, Jay Bryant, Fred G. Burke, Mayor William H. Burlage (Herculaneum, Missouri), Francis M. Burns, Lynne S. Burton, Governor George Busbee (Georgia), E. V. Busch, Edna L. Bush, Harry L. Bush, Ben A. Butler, Clarence L. Busch, Harriet Callahan (Library of Louisiana), Father Leslie F. Chard, Marijane Charlton, H. L. Chiesa, Eschor B. Clewell, Mayor J. R. Closs (Waco, Texas), Luane Cole (Lyme, New

Hampshire, (historian), Mayor Bob Conger (Jackson, Tennessee), Elmer E. Cook, Oscar E. Corde, Lois Costomiris, Gerald K. Coville (town manager, Stockholm, Maine), Mayor Jim Cravens (New Madrid, Missouri), Cecile L. Crosthwait, Bob Crouch, Louis J. Culp, Joyia Culpepper, Steward Daige, J. Deneka, Didney J. Dennis, Frances K. Dent, Dorothy Dodge, T. A. Dodge, Susan E. Donovan, Harry C. Dougherty, Paulina E. Driscoll, Marge Duell, Mayor W. Bruce Dunbar (Zion, Illinois), Mary P. Duston, Winifern Easterday, Edwin Edwards, Virginia L. Elden, E. R. Engle, Governor Daniel J. Evans (Washington), Marcia Farrell, A. B. Fergerson, Vera B. Foss, Fern Foster, Pauline S. Fowler (Jackson County Historical Society, Missouri), Neill W. Freeman, Nelson Fugate, Earl J. Gagnon, Jacqueline Gallup, Thomas A. Gardy, Jr., Margaret B. Garland, Ann Garry, Elmo Gillen, Mrs. John W. Graham, Anna Elizabeth Graming, Mary Grow, Ann Hahn, F. Winfield Haines, Ruth Hall, Thomas E. Hanaway, Mrs. Edward Harland, Mrs. Clinton R. Harris, Catherine Hartang, Lorraine Hayes, F. J. Hays, Margaret L. Hejtmanek, Rose Helmberger, Ruth Wilkirson Henderson, Robert F. Henzoy, Mayor Bobby E. Higgins (Athens, Alabama), Jennie Higgins, M. Hill, Ann Hinckley, W. L. Hobson, Mayor Fred Hofheinz (Houston, Texas), Michael Hornick, Ruth E. Horton, Shirley Hubbard (Lebanon Historical Society, New Hampshire), Michele Hudson, Patricia H. Hudson (Monroe County Historical Commission, Minnesota), Lillian W. Hundley, James N. Hunter, Joan Hunter, William A. Hunter (Pennsylvania Historical and Museum Commission), Curtis R. Jackson (Jackson County Bicentennial Commission, Minnesota), Mary L. James (Gallia County Historical Society, Ohio), Mayor Fred Janke (Jackson, Minnesota), Pauline Jett, Georgia Joachim, Barry H. Johnson, Bettye Johnson, Mayor P. K. Johnson (Refuge, Texas), Helen Jones, Mayor Walter C. Kelly (Shaker Heights, Ohio), Mayor Lester L. Kennedy (Mars, Pennsylvania), Margaret Kennedy (Yates County Historical Society, New York), Mayor Richard A. King (Independence, Missouri), Julia Kinsly (Hancock Historical Society, Vermont), Governor Richard F. Knelp (South Dakota), Kenneth L. Kunde, V. B. Kunz (Ramsey County and Saint Paul Historical Society, Minnesota), Mayor Joseph J. La Roca (Quincy, Maine), Art Lassiter, Bart W. Lahatte, D. Boardman Lee, L. L. Letz, Frances Levasseur, Professor Roy G. Lillard, Mary C. Lipham, S. Longest, James L. Loomis, Jose Luis Lopez, Elsie Lougley, Olive L. Loyd, Governor Patrick J. Lucey (Wisconsin), Madge M. Lutz, Donald R. Mathewson, John W. Matthews, Leo Mazza, G. D. McAndrew, Dorothy McCay, Margie McCollum, Mayor James McCulloch (Fort Fort, Pennsylvania), Marie B. McCutcheon, Marilyn McElrory, Charles M. McGee (Mauch Chunk Historical Society, Pennsylvania), Ernest A.

Meader, Mayor Glen C. Meckfessel (Garfield, Kansas), Martha Merriam, Mayor Frederick Merrin (Amsterdam, Ohio), Betty Murden Michelson, Mrs. G. P. Midyette, Sr., Dorothy Milek, Carol Miller, Governor William G. Milliken (Michigan), Minnesota Historical Society, B. Q. Mixon, Robert G. Moon, Violet Moon, Walter W. Moore, Arcada H. Morgan (Northeast Mississippi Historical Society), William H. Morgan, Mayor W. P. Morton (Perry, Kentucky), Floyd Mullen, Jack Musgrove (Iowa Historical Museum), Ralph A. Nelson, Mayor Thomas Newman (Eminence, Kentucky), Catherine S. Newsom, Jack Norman, Dennis Oase, Ralph Oldham, Gladys Para, Mrs. Randall Parkin, Darlene Pederson, Charles R. Petzke, John R. Platt, Mayor E. B. Pope (Washington, Georgia), Clifford Pryor, Jo Watson Plurius, Ann Rasner, Majorie O'Brien Ratoport (Staten Island Historical Society, New York), Carla Ray, Chester A. Ray, William Allen Reiners (Daviess County Historical Society, Indiana), Catherine B. Remley (Ohio Historical Society), Viola Richey, L. H. Rickard, Mayor Dennis L. Riggin (Devils Lake, North Dakota), Mary S. Robertson, Ralph Roina, Mayor J. Fred Rucker (Dresden, Tennessee), William F. Sammons, Pam Schaub, Mrs. R. A. Shafer, Thomas L. Sharbaugh, Mrs. Leland Sharp (Summit Historical Society, Colorado), Marvin Schumacher, Linda Shepard, Leon Sherwood (Montgomery County Historical Society, Kansas), Elsie M. Sherrill, Marvin Sherrill, Wilbur L. Shutes, Bob Simpson, Kirk Sisson, Dale D. Slater, Mrs. Floyd Smart, Donald L. Smith, M. A. Smith, Nell H. Smith, Wilbur Smith (Texarkana Historical Society, Arkansas–Texas), Joseph A. Sparks, R. M. Stanley, Frances C. Stanzel, J. Morgan Stevens, Robert E. Stewart, Mrs. Ed Stibal, V. M. Stolte, Vernon E. Stoner, Ruth Stumpff, Ruth C. Stuhl, Elsie M. Sullivan, Emil J. Tabaracci, Joe Tarno, Mr. and Mrs. S. H. Taylor, Marty Tharp, Shirley Thayer, Marian Thomson (Mariposa County Historical Society, California), Thomas H. Tippett, Lillian Trittabaugh, Jared Van Wagenen, III, S. A. Ward, June G. Webster, Edna Whittemore, B. Williams. Edmund J. Winslow, Professor Hans Winterfeldt, Jammie Wolfe, Marjorie A. Wule, Kenneth A. Yates, Sue Zache, Devra L. Zetlan.

The editors at Thomas Nelson were invaluable.

My children Michèle and Glenn have earned my loving appreciation and the dedication of this book for the help they eagerly gave in all phases of the work, from research to proofreading.

My wife Iris, through her goodness and her devotion, has created an environment without which this book could not have been written.

A. W.

To Michèle, Glenn, and Brian—
each as unique as the places
within these pages

CONTENTS

BEAUTIFULLY
DIFFERENT

As we travel through the United States we pass signs that announce intriguingly "China, Maine," "Kalamazoo, Michigan," "Napoleonville, Lousiana, and "Chugwater, Wyoming." Thousands of such towns and cities in America have interesting and historical names. You can get a clear picture of what Americans have done and how they have lived just from the names of the places on the map. Over two hundred years of freedom are expressed by many of these names.

Who named these places? Why did the settlers choose the names they did? This book will help answer these questions.

America is a big country with many millions of people. In many ways we are all alike. Most of us speak the same language, wear similar clothing, choose the same products from our supermarket shelves, and watch the same television programs. But in other ways we are beautifully different. We have different ways to pray and different ways to celebrate what we think is important. In many parts of our nation people use different words to describe the same thing. The history of the area that we live in often differs from the history of other American regions. A man living in Maine, for example, has a different kind of pride in his seacoast state from that of a Wyoming cowboy or a tobacco grower from Virginia.

This glorious difference is what makes America the land of the beautiful. The fact that each of us can follow his own path and we can still exist together is the greatness of Columbus' New World.

These differences in our backgrounds, our land, and our people show up in the names that we have given to the places in which we choose to live. These places, with their different names, are monuments to the American free spirit.

AMERICAN STATE NAMES

America

Christopher Columbus made four voyages to the New World between 1492 and 1504. Sailing for Spain, he discovered and explored many parts of the Caribbean region without ever setting foot on what is now the United States.

Seeing what Columbus had done, other sea captains set out from Europe to explore these new discoveries. One of these was a Florentine (Italian) seaman named Amerigo Vespucci. After his voyage, he wrote letters to important people in Europe telling them about the great new continent. Amerigo's fame was ensured when a noted mapmaker put his name on the New World section of a widely used map. In time, this part of the earth became known as America.

A century later, the major powers of Europe began to send settlers across the Atlantic to colonize the promising land. Soon, the central part of the North American continent was claimed by the three most powerful European countries—Spain took the south and west, England the east and central area, and France the north and midcontinent (Mississippi Valley). However, the French lost their hold on Canada and Louisiana in the French and Indian War, and with the advent of the American Revolution in 1775, possession of the central region passed to the new United States of America. Within the next seventy-five years Spain's lands, too, became part of the American colossus.

Since then these lands have been reshaped into fifty different states, each unique in its own way, whether because of its land, its people, or its history.

The names that have been given to these parcels of land, and hence to the people who live within them, tell us a great deal about Americans. Half of all states have names that are derived from what the Indians called their land. Nine states have taken the names of the main rivers that flow through them. Others are named after important people, the geography of the region, or names that came about through common usage.

Each state name has a story behind it that provides us a glimpse into its past. Together, these fifty names give a unique picture of an important part of American history.

Alabama

THE NAME

Alabama, or Alibamu, was the name of a southern Indian tribe in the central section of this state. These Indians, part of the Creek Confederacy, lived on a river bearing the same name. Some say that the Choctaw word *alabama* means "thicket clearers," signifying that the people cleared weeds and other vegetation from the land in order to grow food.

SPOTLIGHT ON HISTORY

More than four hundred years ago this area was the scene of several Spanish explorations. In 1540, Hernando de Soto, accompanied by well-armed soldiers, marched through here in search of gold. His presence was not welcomed by Choctaw chief Tuscaloosa, who engaged in an all-out battle with the European intruders. According to Spanish sources, 2,500 Indians were killed.

Later, France settled part of the region, followed by England. In 1783 England ceded the territory to the United States, a result of her defeat in the American Revolution.

IMPORTANT DATES
1540—Hernando de Soto explores the area for Spain.
1702—French build Fort Louis de la Mobile.
1763—Britain acquires Alabama land from France.

1783—Area ceded to the United States by Britain in treaty ending the American Revolution.

1814—Creek Indians are defeated by General Andrew Jackson in the Battle of Horseshoe Bend.

1819—Alabama is admitted as the twenty-second state.

Alaska

THE NAME

This land of the midnight sun got its name from the Aleut word *alaschka*, which means "mainland" or "great land." This description was used by the people who lived on the nearby Aleutian Islands.

SPOTLIGHT ON HISTORY

Sailing for Russia, Vitus Bering was commissioned to find out if there was a northeast passage through the Arctic to India and China. His sponsor, Czar Peter the Great, also wanted to know if Asia and America were joined. Bering discovered no physical connection, but in 1728 he did claim for Russia what was eventually to become the largest and most northern American state. The Bering Strait between Russia and Alaska, which he also discovered, is named for him.

On October 18, 1867, 139 years after Bering's first voyage, President Andrew Johnson reluctantly followed the advice of his Secretary of State, William H. Seward, and bought the Russian territory for the bargain price of $7.2 million. It was one of the greatest real-estate deals in history—second only to the purchase of Louisiana from France for $16 million. The derisively nicknamed Seward's Icebox added more than 500,000 square miles to the United States at less than two cents an acre.

THE LAND AND THE PEOPLE

This huge state, twice the size of Texas, has no fewer than six different climatic and geographic areas, ranging from hot, damp rain forests to windy, frozen tundras. It has innumerable lakes, many active volcanoes, and gargantuan glaciers. One glacier, Malaspina, is larger than the state of Rhode Island.

Originally three groups of people lived there—Eskimos, Indians, and Aleuts. Today these natives number about 60,000, more than half being Eskimos.

IMPORTANT DATES

1728—Vitus Bering sails near area of Alaska, discovers strait.

1741—Bering lands on Alaskan mainland.

1784—First European settlement is made by Russians on Kodiak Island; area henceforth known as Russian America.

1867—United States buys "Seward's Icebox" and changes name to Alaska.

1880—Gold is discovered.

1896—Famous gold strike in neighboring Yukon brings influx of sourdough prospectors.

1957—Oil is discovered in Kenai Peninsula.

1959—Alaska becomes the forty-ninth state.

1973—Trans-Alaska pipeline is authorized to bring petroleum from the North Slope.

Arizona

THE NAME

Around 1735 a great silver strike was made at a spot where small springs were located. The Pima Indians called them *Arishoonak*, which meant "little spring place." The Spanish referred to them as *Arizonac*, and this later became Arizona. As it turned out, the springs did not become part of the state of Arizona, but are in Sonora, Mexico.

When New Mexico asked Congress to create what was to become the Arizona territory, that august body considered names to call it—Pimeria, Gadsonia, and Arizona. The latter won, because, among other reasons, it sounded best to the ear.

SPOTLIGHT ON HISTORY

The Grand Canyon State, home of ancient, advanced Indian cultures, was explored and settled by Spain as far back as the middle of the sixteenth century. In 1540, Francisco de Coronado led a military force deep into this arid region looking for the fabled Seven Cities of Cibola, which were supposed to have many golden treasures. Coronado gave up after two years of fruitless searching, but the Spaniards liked the land and established numerous missions there during the next century.

The area later became part of Mexico when that country gained its independence from Spain in 1821. The United States acquired it as a result of the Mexican War and the Gadsden Purchase.

IMPORTANT DATES

1540—Coronado explores parts of Arizona.

1690—Spain begins building missions.

1821—Mexico wins her independence from Spain, taking Arizona with her.

1848—United States seizes most of Arizona at end of Mexican War.

1854—Gadsden Purchase gives United States the rest of Arizona land.

1912—Arizona becomes the forty-eighth state.

Arkansas

THE NAME

French Jesuits, exploring this area, came upon a tribe called Ugakhpa (Quapaws), which were called Oo-ka-na-sa pronounced by the Algonkian Indians. One of the Jesuits, Jacques Marquette, recorded the name Arkansea, meaning "downstream people," on his map in 1673.

The region became a territory in 1819 with the name Arkansaw, an American spelling for a French pronunciation. The territory was admitted into the Union as the state of Arkansas. In later years, by special edict, the name was officially pronounced *Ark*-an-saw. (However, the river of the same name, which runs through the state, is pronounced Ar-*kan*sas, like the state of Kansas.)

SPOTLIGHT ON HISTORY

Arkansas was another part of the North American continent that the Spaniards explored in search of gold. Here, Hernando de Soto looked in vain for the precious metal during the years 1541 and 1542. A century later French explorers descended on the land, claiming it for France as part of the vast territory—all lands watered by the Mississippi and Missouri rivers— they called Louisiana. The territory then changed hands several times, going to Spain, then back to France. Finally, in 1803, President Thomas Jefferson made his famous Louisiana Purchase, and Arkansas became part of the United States. It was admitted to the Union in 1836.

Arkansas commemorates having been ruled by Spain, France, and the United States, with a star for each of them on its state flag. There is also a larger star signifying the years it belonged to the Confederacy.

IMPORTANT DATES
1541—De Soto explores for Spain.
1673—Marquette and Joliet travel down the Mississippi River to the mouth of the Arkansas.
1682—Mississippi Valley is claimed for France by La Salle.
1762—France cedes region to Spain.
1800—Region reverts to France.
1803—The United States buys Louisiana Territory from France for $16 million, doubling its size.
1836—Arkansas becomes the twenty-fifth state.

California

THE NAME

In the early 1500's a succession of Spanish expeditions to the southern and northern portions of this coastal territory gave it the name "California." The explorers Cortez and Cabrillo apparently had read Ordoñez de Montalvo's novel, *Las Sergas de Esplandián*, in which the author wrote:

Know then, that west of the Indies, but to the east of Eden, lies California, an island peopled by a swarthy, robust, passionate race of women living manless like Amazons. Their island, the most rugged in the world, abounds in gold. Having no other metal, all their armor and weapons are made of this gold.

The fictional island "California" and its ruler, "Queen Calafia" were figments of Señor Montalvo's active imagination—in all probability, coined words.

SPOTLIGHT ON HISTORY

California has had a colorful history, beginning with Spanish exploration and settlement in its southern part and British and Russian claims to its northern region. Mexico took over in 1821, upon winning its freedom from Spain. Mexican rule didn't last long. Twenty-five years later, American settlers in this territory revolted and set up the independent Bear Flag Republic. Their new country was also short-lived, however, being occupied by United States troops twenty-six days later. That was during the Mexican War. The Pacific State was officially acquired with the signing of the peace treaty of Guadalupe Hidalgo in 1848.

Shortly before the treaty was signed, gold had been discovered by James W. Marshall at Sutter's Mill. California was soon to become a boom state. During the next few years hundreds of thousands of people flocked from all parts of the world seeking their fortunes.

The importance of this mineral in California's early history is indicated in several of its official symbols:

State motto: "Eureka!" (I have found it!)
State nickname: The Golden State.
State colors: blue and gold.
State mineral: native gold.
State fish: golden trout.
State flower: golden poppy.

IMPORTANT DATES

1542—Juan Cabrillo explores lower California coast for Spain.
1579—Francis Drake takes possession of northern California coastal land for England.
1769—Spanish settle at San Diego and San Francisco Bay.
1822—The province of California declares allegiance to Mexico.
1846—Bear Flag Republic is formed in California.
1848—Gold is discovered at Sutter's Mill, and the United States acquires California from Mexico.
1850—California becomes the thirty-first state.

Carolina
North and South

THE NAME

This region was given the name "Carolina" at different periods of time for three different European monarchs—the French King Charles IX and the English Kings Charles I and Charles II. In 1629 Charles I granted his attorney general, Sir Robert Heath, this area, writing: "and we name it Carolana, or Province of Carolana, and the said islands, Islands of Carolana, and so for all time hereafter we wish them to be called."

In 1690, the colony was divided into two sections and administered separately, and in 1712 these sections were formally separated into the colonies of North and South Carolina.

During the American Revolution, North Carolina was nicknamed the "Tar Heel State." This came about, according to legend, when the troops of British General Cornwallis got their feet blackened crossing a river that had tar dumped into it. They commented bitterly that anyone wading through North Carolina streams would wind up with tar heels.

SPOTLIGHT ON HISTORY

The Spanish and the French made unsuccessful attempts to establish settlements in the Carolinas. The British profited from the experiences of their predecessors, successfully planting a colony there in 1663.

Both Carolinas were active participants in America's early wars. In 1773 a group of North Carolina ladies, for example, held the Edenton Tea Party—a meeting that vowed to boycott English tea. When the war began, both states sent thousands of troops to battle the English, the Tories, and the Cherokee Indians.

On December 20, 1860, South Carolina became the first southern state to secede from the Union. North Carolina, on the other hand, was the last, not seceding until May 20, 1861.

IMPORTANT DATES

1629—Charles I grants land to Sir Robert Heath.

1663—Charles II grants charter to eight English noblemen as proprietors.

1690—Carolina is divided into two administrative divisions.

1712—North and South Carolina become two separate colonies.

1729—Both Carolinas become royal provinces, no longer run by proprietors.

1776—Carolinas declare their independence from Great Britain.

1788—On May 23 South Carolina ratifies the Constitution, becoming the eighth state to do so.

1789—On November 21 North Carolina ratifies, becoming the twelfth state.

Colorado

THE NAME

In 1602 a Spanish expedition named a stream in this area *Colorado*, a word which described the reddish color of the water, acquired by flowing through canyons of red stone. The name was later used for the region's main body of water, the Colorado River, and then for the territory and state. Previously known as the Grand River, the Colorado River was officially given its name forty-five years after the territory became a state.

SPOTLIGHT ON HISTORY

The Colorado land came from several United States' acquisitions: the Louisiana Purchase in 1803, the Texas Annexation in 1845, and the Mexican Cession in 1848.

In 1806, a large party, headed by Zebulon Pike, thoroughly explored the region, bringing back word of the beautiful land and the promise it offered. A large peak that they came upon has been named in Pike's honor.

Thereafter, rapid settlement of the Centennial State began, spurred on by the Mexican Cession, the discovery of gold, and completion of a railroad line to Denver.

IMPORTANT DATES
1803 — Eastern Colorado becomes part of the United States as a result of Louisiana Purchase.
1806 — Pike explores the area.
1848 — Western Colorado becomes part of the United States as a result of Mexican War.
1858 — Gold is discovered.
1861 — Colorado Territory is created.
1870 — Denver Pacific and Kansas Pacific railroads are completed.
1876 — Colorado is admitted as the thirty-eighth state.

Connecticut

THE NAME

Connecticut is one of several states that acquired their names from a main river flowing through them. The Algonkians called the body of water *KwEnihtEkot*, meaning "long tidal river." The colony, and later the state, took its name from the Connecticut River.

SPOTLIGHT ON HISTORY

Settlement began in earnest after the defeat of the coastal Pequot Indians in the Pequot War of 1637. Two years later, Puritans from the Massachusetts Bay Colony joined with another group to form a new community and to create America's first written constitution—the Fundamental Orders of Connecticut. Nearby, other Puritans established a settlement that they called New Haven, a home that they hoped would be a haven from religious persecution.

The colonies were put on a sound basis in 1662 when Charles II granted them a legal charter, which contained an unusual degree of self-government.

IMPORTANT DATES

1614—Connecticut River explored by Adriaen Block of the Dutch West India Company.

1633—The river towns of Windsor, Wethersfield, and Hartford are settled.

1637—The Pequot Indians are defeated and massacred.

1638—New Haven is founded.

1662—Royal charter is granted.

1788—Connecticut is fifth state to ratify the Constitution.

Dakota
North and South

THE NAME

Dakota is the Sioux Indian word for "friend" or "ally." It became
the name for each of these territories when they were established in 1861.
During their twenty-eight years under territorial status, the two regions
competed for this name. When statehood was finally granted, they settled
their rivalry with the North and South compromise. They were jointly
admitted into the Union on November 2, 1889, President Benjamin Harrison signing the legal documents in such a way that it was not known
which state was admitted first.

SPOTLIGHT ON HISTORY

Pierre de La Vérendrye, a French explorer, was the first European to
visit the northern part of this area. In 1738 he sought but never found a
shorter route to the Pacific Ocean. Five years later, his sons François and
Louis-Joseph explored the southern region, which strengthened France's
claim to the Louisiana Territory. The land then changed hands three
times—to Spain, back to France, and then to the United states for the
bargain price of $16 million. Shortly thereafter, the famous exploring
team of Lewis and Clark charted the region, in preparation for the hordes
of settlers that would come in the decades ahead.

As the white man moved in, native Indian tribes, especially the
Sioux, were pushed, year after year, into smaller and smaller areas of
South Dakota. General George Custer's total defeat at the Battle of the
Little Bighorn was the aftermath of efforts by the Sioux to keep gold
prospectors away from the Black Hills, the last piece of land guaranteed
them.

Indian resistance was finally ended in 1890 at the infamous
Wounded Knee massacre, where government troops slaughtered unarmed
Indian men, women, and children because they refused to stop practicing
a ceremony that the white settlers were unduly alarmed about—the religious Ghost Dance.

IMPORTANT DATES
1738—Vérendrye explores northern Dakota.
1743—Vérendrye's sons explore southern Dakota.
1803—France sells Louisiana Territory, of which Dakota is a part.
1804-05—Lewis and Clark explore Louisiana Territory.
1861—Dakota Territories are created by Congress.
1876—Custer defeated at Battle of the Little Bighorn.
1889—North and South Dakota are admitted as the thirty-ninth and for-
       tieth states.
1890—Indians are massacred at Wounded Knee, South Dakota, during
       the Messiah War.

Delaware

THE NAME

In 1610 Captain Samuel Argall was blown off course near a cape in this region. He immediately named it for his sponsor, Lord De La Warr, the first governor of Virginia. The name was later applied to the area's bay, river, Indian tribe, and colony.

SPOTLIGHT ON HISTORY

Delaware, during the first half of the seventeenth century, was the scene of colonization battles between Holland and Sweden. The British entered in 1664 to take all the Dutch territory in America.

This area was inhabited by the Lenni Lenape (Delaware) Indians well before any of the colonists arrived. They were revered by other regional tribes, who gave them the honored title "Grandfathers." William Penn was quite impressed with these natives who, he said, were "proper and shapely, very swift, their language lofty. They speak little, but fervently and with great elegancy. I have never seen more natural sagacity. . . ."

IMPORTANT DATES
1609—Delaware Bay and River are explored by Henry Hudson.
1631—First European settlement (Dutch) is established.
1638—Swedes settle at what is now Wilmington.
1664—English conquer New Netherlands and rename it New York.

1682—Duke of York deeds Delaware counties to William Penn.

1787—On December 7, Delaware becomes the first state to ratify the Constitution.

Florida

THE NAME

According to Herrera, historian to the King of Spain, Ponce de Leon and his crew,

> believing that land to be an island, they nam'd it *Florida*, because it appear'd very delightful, having many pleasant groves, and it was all level; as also because they discovered it at Easter, which as has been said, the Spaniards call *Pasqua de Flores*, or *Florida*.

It was customary for Spanish explorers to name an area for the day on which it was discovered.

SPOTLIGHT ON HISTORY

Beginning with Luis Ponce de Leon in 1513, Spanish explorers probed deeply into the Florida wilderness. Señor Ponce de Leon did not find the gold he sought or the "fountains of youth" that legend says he looked for. On his second voyage to Florida, eight years later, he was mortally wounded by an Indian arrow. Hernando de Soto, another famous conquistador to visit Florida, also found death and not gold on his American journey. Despite these mishaps, Spain was able to place a colony in Florida, which was named St. Augustine. It is the oldest surviving European city in the United States.

After numerous wars among Spain, France, and England, Florida was ceded to Great Britain in 1763. Twenty years later it was given back to Spain, which in turn sold it to the United States in 1821.

IMPORTANT DATES

1513—Ponce de Leon claims and names Florida for Spain.

1539—De Soto explores Tampa area of Florida.

1565—St. Augustine is settled.

1763—Britain acquires East and West Florida from Spain.

1783—Florida colonies are returned to Spain.

1821—United States purchases Florida.
1845—Florida becomes the twenty-seventh state.

Georgia

THE NAME

In 1732 James Oglethorpe was granted a charter from George II for the creation of a colony in this part of the New World. It was intended as a place of refuge and a fresh start for unfortunates and debtors. The following year, Oglethorpe sailed on the ship *Anne* and set up a community along the Savannah River. The new colony was named in honor of his king.

SPOTLIGHT ON HISTORY

Georgia was the last of the thirteen English colonies to be founded and as such had a population that was strongly loyal to the mother country. Thus, at the time of the American Revolution, there was great friction between these Loyalists (or Tories) and the Georgia faction that was for independence—the Whigs. They engaged in combat with each other on many occasions.

GEORGIA AND WOMEN'S RIGHTS
1802—First woman to own and edit a newspaper, *The Washington Gazette* (Sarah Porter Hillhouse).
1819—First women's foreign missionary society.
1836—First college in the world chartered to grant a degree to women (Wesleyan College at Macon).
1866—First state to declare that married women should have full property rights (Married Women's Act).
1912—Girl Scouts of America founded by Juliette Low.
1922—First woman U.S. Senator (Rebecca Felton).

OTHER IMPORTANT DATES
1540—Hernando de Soto leads Spanish expedition across Georgia territory.
1732—Colony charter is granted to James Oglethorpe by George II.
1788—On January 2, Georgia becomes the fourth state to ratify the Constitution.

Hawaii

THE NAME

The word *hawaii* is Polynesian for "homeland," with *hawa* meaning "place of residence" and *ii* meaning "smaller" or "new." These beautiful Pacific islands may have acquired their name from the navigator Hawaii Loa, who is believed to have discovered them.

During one period of time they were called the Sandwich Islands, so named by Captain James Cook for the Earl of Sandwich, First Lord of the British Admiralty. This was protested by Hawaiian King Kamehameha I, who said that each island should be known by its own name and the entire chain called Islands of the King of Hawaii.

The main Hawaiian Islands are Hawaii, Maui, Oahu, Kauai, Molokai, Lanai, Niihau, and Kahoolawe.

SPOTLIGHT ON HISTORY

More than one thousand years ago, people from a region of the South Seas traveled across the Pacific waters to settle here. The Hawaiian Islands were ruled in the 1800's by a succession of intelligent and beneficent rulers, Kings Kamehameha I to the V. During this time, there was progressive intervention by foreign powers in the affairs of the monarchs and their state. By 1893, American missionaries and businessmen, who had vested interests in the islands, grew concerned about the power of the new monarch, Queen Liliuokalani. She was soon overthrown by a group of Americans, who then set up their own self-styled republic. Five years later the islands were annexed by the United States.

THE LAND AND THE PEOPLE

Polynesians migrated from the Asian shore to islands such as Tahiti and the Marquesas before they settled on the Hawaii Islands. Full-blooded Polynesians, numbering 350,000 in the 1770's, have dwindled to fewer than 10,000 today—a result of disease and intermarriage. Approximately half of the present population is of Asian background, with 30 percent of these from southern Japan and Okinawa. Another 25 percent consists of Caucasians, or *haoles*, as they are referred to by the Oriental population.

IMPORTANT DATES

A.D. 750—Polynesian people from the South Seas settle in Hawaii.
1778—British Captain James Cook discovers the Hawaiian chain and names it the Sandwich Islands.
1810—King Kamehameha I unites and rules all islands in the archipelago.
1820—New England missionaries arrive in Hawaii, teach the population to read and write.
1893—Group of American residents overthrows the monarchy.
1898—Hawaii is annexed by the United States.
1941—Pearl Harbor is attacked by Japan on December 7, precipitating the United States into World War II.
1959—Hawaii is admitted as the fiftieth state.

Idaho

THE NAME

The name *Idaho* means "salmon tribe" or "salmon eaters." There was so much salmon in this region that local Shoshonean Indians were called the Idaho or Salmon tribe.

In 1860 a spokesman for the area's mining interests suggested that Congress call the new territory "Idaho," because he mistakenly believed it meant "gem of the mountains." Congress agreed, but at the last minute changed the name to Colorado, because they, also mistakenly, thought *Idaho* was not an Indian word. A group of people who preferred the name Idaho began to organize and apply pressure. Joseph Ruckel, for example, named his newly launched Columbia River steamboat *Idaho*, as did the owners of the newly opened Clearwater and Salmon River gold mines. It worked. In 1863 the new territory was officially named Idaho.

SPOTLIGHT ON HISTORY

Idaho was another part of the great Louisiana Purchase that Lewis and Clark explored in 1805. The discovery of gold at Weippe in 1860 brought a horde of prospectors, followed by farmers who knew they could profit by the inflated prices their products would bring. The Indians suffered here, as they did in other parts of the United States, when white men broke treaties and stole their land. They fought back, notably in the 1877 Nez Percé War. The courageous Nez Percé leader, Chief Joseph, then took his people on a long journey, seeking to cross the border into Canada. He was stopped by government troops just a few miles short of his goal.

IMPORTANT DATES
1805—Lewis and Clark explore Idaho on their way to the Pacific.
1860—Gold is discovered.
1863—Idaho Territory is created.
1890—Idaho becomes the forty-third state.

Illinois

THE NAME

Illinois is a French corruption of a word in the language of the Illini Indians, which means either "men," "warriors," or "persons of the Illinois tribe." In 1679, a French explorer, Robert de La Salle, traveled down the river that traverses this region and called the Indians who lived along its banks the Illinois.

SPOTLIGHT ON HISTORY

Several European countries—Spain, England, and France—made early claims on this part of the Louisiana Territory. French settlement began after the explorers Marquette and Jolliet sent word back to France of the rich soil and the unexcelled wildlife that they had seen there. France, however, was forced to cede the land to England in 1763 after her defeat in the French and Indian War. Remaining French settlers later had some revenge on the British by helping the Americans during the War for Independence.

In the next century, Illinois was the scene of another important battle, the political fight between Abraham Lincoln and Stephen A. Douglas for their state's Senate seat. Douglas won the contest, because his compromise doctrine allowed new territories to choose whether or not they wanted slavery within their boundaries. The defeated Lincoln nevertheless made his name as a skilled debater by taking the opposite view and thus became a popular figure in many parts of the country. He went on to lead the antislavery Republican Party to Presidential victory in 1860.

Indiana

THE NAME

The presence of Indians in this section of the United States inspired a land development company to call their holdings "Indiana." The name was used for the territory in 1800 and later for the state.

The people here are nicknamed "Hoosiers," which came about, according to folklore, when the early pioneers used to greet nightcallers by saying, "Who's yere?"

SPOTLIGHT ON HISTORY

The Miami, Delaware, and Pottawattomi were some of the many tribes who lived in this area. The Indians, resenting that European countries and white settlers were taking over their lands, engaged in a long series of battles with the intruders. They sided with the French against the British in the French and Indian Wars and later successfully rebelled against the British and held them off for a year in what was known as Pontiac's War. Twice in the 1790's they defeated American forces sent against them, until finally, on August 12, 1794, they were overcome by the troops of General "Mad Anthony" Wayne in the Battle of Fallen Timbers (near Maumee). Their last efforts to obtain justice were made in the early 1800's under the leadership of the Shawnee chief Tecumseh. His forces were defeated by William Henry Harrison at the famous Battle of Tippecanoe, November 7, 1811, and Tecumseh himself was killed two years later in Ontario.

1794—Indians are defeated at the Battle of Fallen Timbers.
1816—Indiana becomes the nineteenth state.

Iowa

THE NAME

This was an Indian tribal name which has gone through the following stages of spelling and pronunciation: *Quaouiatonon* to *Ouaouia* to *Iowa*. The name means "one who puts to sleep," and may refer to the Iowa Indians' ability to put visitors and others to sleep, perhaps through hypnotism. The name Iowa was given to the area's main river and then to the territory and state.

SPOTLIGHT ON HISTORY

This was another part of the North American continent that was widely traversed by French explorers. Jacques Marquette and Louis Jolliet penetrated in the 1670's. The other famous exploration team, Lewis and Clark, delved into Iowa's inner regions after President Jefferson purchased the Louisiana Territory in 1803.

For the next thirty years the future breadbasket of America was Indian land, not officially open for settlement. This situation ended as a result of the 1832 Black Hawk War, after which the Indian lands in Iowa were rapidly turned over to white settlers. It is interesting that Iowa later took its nickname, the Hawkeye State, from the same Sauk chief, Black Hawk, who was defeated in that war.

IMPORTANT DATES
1673—Marquette and Jolliet explore area.
1682—Louisiana region is claimed by La Salle for France.
1762—France cedes land to Spain.
1800—Spain secretly returns area to France.
1803—The United States buys Louisiana Territory, which includes Iowa.
1820—Slavery is prohibited in Iowa by the Missouri Compromise.
1838—Iowa Territory is created by Congress.
1846—Iowa becomes the twenty-ninth state.

Kansas

THE NAME

This was another of the many names that advanced from Indian tribe to river to name of territory and then to official state name. The KaNze tribe (a word meaning "the south wind") lived in this area near the river that eventually bore their name. The present *Kansas* is a French spelling with an English pronunciation of the final *s*.

SPOTLIGHT ON HISTORY

Spanish conquistador Francisco Vasquez de Coronado searched this area in his frustrated attempt to find the nonexisting Seven Golden Cities of Cibola. He found no gold, but he did describe the area as "the best I have ever seen for producing all the products of Spain."

Others apparently agreed with his estimation of the worth of Kansas, because, three centuries later, both proslavery and antislavery factions struggled to get control of this newly settled region. They came here under the provisions of the 1854 Kansas-Nebraska Act, which permitted the residents of these two territories to decide for themselves whether slavery would be allowed in their regions. This led to pitched battles between the two groups, which climaxed in the bloody raids of May, 1856, on Lawrence and Pottawatomie. The area well earned its grim nickname "Bleeding Kansas." Kansas was finally admitted to the Union as a free state in 1861.

KANSAS AND WOMEN'S RIGHTS

1861—State Constitution gives equal privileges to women in ownership of property and in control of their children and grants women suffrage in school elections.

1887—World's first woman mayor (Medora Salter of Argonia) is elected.

1912—State constitutional amendment gives women full suffrage.

OTHER IMPORTANT DATES

1541—Coronado explores area for Spain.

1804—Lewis and Clark expedition crosses Kansas.

1854—Kansas-Nebraska Act allows settlers in these territories to decide for or against slavery.
1861—Kansas becomes the thirty-fourth state.

Kentucky

THE NAME

Kentucky or *kentake* was an Iroquoian word which meant "plain" or "meadowland." Kentucky was part of Virginia until it became a state in 1792, soon after adoption of the United States Constitution.

SPOTLIGHT ON HISTORY

The history of Kentucky and Daniel Boone are closely tied together.

In 1769 Boone and several others went into Kentucky to explore and hunt. They remained for almost two years. Boone went back again in 1775, this time as an agent for the Transylvania Land Company, which commissioned the frontiersman to blaze a trail across the Cumberland Gap to Kentucky. A major part of his work was to establish a settlement, which he called Boonesborough, on the Kentucky River.

However, settling the land was made extremely difficult because of constant Indian attacks. The year 1777, called the Year of the Three Seven's by the white settlers, was an especially grueling one. Boone and his new community were constantly involved in Indian skirmishes. One day Boone was captured by an Indian war party while he and some men were boiling salt at Blue Licks. He was taken to Fort Detroit, where he was held and later adopted by Chief Blackfish of the Shawnee. This was not for Boone. He soon escaped and in an epic run—160 miles in four days—he made his way back to Boonesborough in time to help repel a massive Indian assault.

IMPORTANT DATES
1769—Daniel Boone crosses the Cumberland Gap into Kentucky.
1774—First permanent settlement is made at Harrodstown.
1775—Treaty of Sycamore Shoals is signed with Cherokee Indians—opening part of Kentucky for settlement; Boone blazes trail to Kentucky and founds Boonesborough.
1777—Year of fierce Indian attacks plagues settlers.
1792—Kentucky becomes the fifteenth state.

Louisiana

THE NAME

In 1682 Robert de La Salle named the immense area, of which this state was a small part, "Louisiane," in honor of Louis XIV of France.

SPOTLIGHT ON HISTORY

Ten flags have flown over Louisiana during different times in its history: the Spanish flag of Leon and Castile; the French royal Fleur-de-Lis; the red and white flag of Bourbon Spain; the British Union Jack; the tricolor of the French Republic; the American fifteen-stripe flag; the Lone Star flag of the West Florida Republic; the Confederate Stars and Bars; the flag of independent Louisiana; and the present Stars and Stripes.

This international exchange of land has had a cultural effect on Louisiana. You can find, for example, Spanish contributions in architecture and the legal system, and use of the French language by numerous families around the region of New Orleans. Southern Louisiana has a large group of French Canadian descendants, called Cajuns—a corruption of Acadian, from the part of French Canada where they originated—who speak pidgin French, a language that also contains some English, German, Spanish, and Indian words.

IMPORTANT DATES
1541—De Soto explores the Mississippi River.
1682—Louisiana Territory is claimed for France.
1714—First permanent settlement is made.
1762—France cedes Louisiana to Spain.
1800—Spain returns Louisiana to France.
1803—Louisiana Territory is purchased by President Jefferson for $16 million, doubling the area of the United States.
1812—Louisiana becomes the eighteenth state.

Maine

THE NAME

Early explorers, distinguishing between the islands and the mainland in this part of New England, referred to this section of land as "the maine." This common usage became its official name when it was separated from Massachusetts to become the twenty-third state.

SPOTLIGHT ON HISTORY

Many explorers, including John and Sebastian Cabot, visited this stretch of land on the Atlantic coastline. In the early 1600's both the French and British attempted to plant small colonies here, the latter failing. Massachusetts, seventy years later, purchased the province of Maine, maintaining control until this land to the north was made a sovereign state.

Maine's statehood was the result of a Congressional agreement between the Northern and Southern states, historically called the Missouri Compromise of 1820. A key provision of that law balanced the admittance of Missouri, a slave state, with that of Maine, a free state.

IMPORTANT DATES

1598-99—John and Sebastian Cabot explore Maine coast, stopping to view area.

1604—French plant a colony on St. Croix Island.

1607—Unsuccessful British settlement at the mouth of the Sagadahoc (now Kennebec) River.

1677—Massachusetts purchases all of Maine province from heirs of Sir Ferdinando Gorges.

1820—Missouri Compromise enables Maine to be admitted as the twenty-third state.

Maryland

THE NAME

Many explorers named new lands after their kings, and several kings gave this high honor to their queens. King Charles I of England suggested that this colony's founder, Cecil Calvert, Lord Baltimore, name it *Terra Mariae*, "Mary's Land," for his queen Henrietta Maria. She was the daughter of Henry IV of France.

SPOTLIGHT ON HISTORY

In 1608 John Smith from Jamestown was the first European to explore the harbors and islands of the great Chesapeake Bay—two hundred miles long. In 1634 a colony was founded at St. Mary's as the first religious refuge in the New World.

Two centuries later, Maryland and Virginia volunteered portions of their land for the creation of a national capital to be known as the District of Columbia. Virginia later got her territory back, thus leaving the entire capital composed of former Maryland terrain.

Maryland once again came into the spotlight in 1814 when British troops and naval squadrons attempted to land and burn Baltimore. During the bombardment of Fort McHenry, which protected the city's harbor, a Washington lawyer named Francis Scott Key wrote "The Star Spangled Banner."

IMPORTANT DATES

1608—John Smith charts Chesapeake Bay.

1632—Colony charter issued to the second Lord Baltimore by Charles I.

1649—Maryland assembly passes the Act Concerning Religion, the world's first official guarantee of freedom of worship (it was later nullified by the crown).

1788—On April 28, Maryland ratifies the Constitution, becoming the seventh state.

1791—Maryland cedes sixty-nine and a quarter square miles to the federal government to become the District of Columbia.

Massachusetts

THE NAME

An Algonkian Indian village got the name *Mes-atsu-s-et*, meaning "large hill place," from the fact that it was located in the region of the Great Blue Hill, near what is now Boston. The name was later applied to the tribe and then to the American colony.

SPOTLIGHT ON HISTORY

It is believed that Leif Ericson and his Norsemen may have visited this area around A.D. 1000. This was 620 years before the Pilgrims anchored the *Mayflower* to establish the colony of Plymouth. These 101 Pilgrims had landed in an area that was beyond the boundaries of their original land grant, hence the governance rules of the old charter did not apply. Thus, they created their own society agreement, the Mayflower Compact, an original document that provided for majority rule.

This gallant little group barely survived the first grueling winter, which left half of them dead. The others, aided by friendly Indians, struggled through. Soon more colonists came, and Plymouth Rock, Massachusetts, became a landmark in American history.

MASSACHUSETTS FIRSTS

1621—First American Thanksgiving celebrated (Plymouth).

1635—First American public secondary school (Boston).

1636—First American university (Harvard).

1639—First American post office (Boston).

1644—First free American elementary school.

1653—First American public library (Boston).

1775—First battle of the Revolution (Lexington–Concord).

1789—First American novel published (William Hill Brown, *The Power of Sympathy*).

1845—First sewing machine made (Elias Howe, Boston).

1875—First American Christmas card printed (Boston).

1876—First telephone demonstrated (Alexander Graham Bell, Boston).

1891—First basketball game played (Springfield).

1898—First American subway system (Boston).

1926—First successful liquid-fuel rocket launched (Dr. Robert Goddard, Auburn).

1928—First computer developed (Dr. Vannevar Bush, MIT).

OTHER IMPORTANT DATES

A.D. *1000*—Norsemen were believed to have visited area.

1614—Coast is explored and described by Captain John Smith.

1620—Pilgrims land at Plymouth Rock.

1629—Massachusetts Bay Company receives royal charter from Charles I.

1788—On January 6, Massachusetts becomes the sixth state to ratify the Constitution.

Michigan

THE NAME

The Chippewa word *majiigan* means "large clearing." An Indian tribe in the area lived in such a location and was thus named the Michigans. The name was later given to Lake Michigan and then to the territory and state.

SPOTLIGHT ON HISTORY

The fur trade was the main reason for French and British rivalry in this area. Britain gained control over Canada in 1763 and maintained possession of the Great Lakes region for the next thirty-three years.

During this entire exploration and settlement period, the Indians struggled to get their land back, siding with whichever European power that would help them. In early days they supported the French against the British; in 1763, under the Ottawa chief Pontiac, they organized a powerful assault on Britain's frontier forts; then in the Revolution and the War of 1812, they aided the British against the Americans.

Michigan was admitted to the Union as a free state in a Senate compromise that simultaneously admitted the slave state of Arkansas.

IMPORTANT DATES

1634—French begin 130 years of occupation.

1763—Treaty of Paris gives Britain all of Canada and the Great Lakes area. Pontiac revolts and lays siege to Fort Detroit.

1794—General Anthony Wayne defeats Indians at Fallen Timbers, ending Indian attacks on backwoods settlements.
1796—British finally evacuate American territory.
1837—Michigan becomes the twenty-sixth state.

Minnesota

THE NAME

Minnesota, like eight other states (Colorado, Connecticut, Illinois, Mississippi, Nebraska, Ohio, Oregon, and Wisconsin), got its name from a river flowing through it. The river, a western tributary of the great Mississippi, had been known during an earlier time by the Sioux name *Mnishota*—"milky" or "clouded" water. This was changed by the French to Rivière de Saint Pierre—"St. Peter's River," which it was called for 150 years. It took a special act of Congress in 1852 to change it back to its original name.

SPOTLIGHT ON HISTORY

In the seventeenth century, French explorers entered the region seeking a shorter route to the Pacific and the riches of Cathay. They were soon followed into this Mississippi Valley wilderness by fur traders and missionaries, all eager to succeed in their tasks.

Britain replaced France here in 1763 and, despite her treaties with the United States after the Revolution and the War of 1812, still controlled parts of the territory for several years thereafter.

IMPORTANT DATES
1669—French enter Minnesota region.
1763—British acquire territory from France.
1783—Minnesota East is ceded to the United States at the end of the Revolution.
1803—Minnesota West becomes American territory as part of the Louisiana Purchase.
1858—Minnesota becomes the thirty-second state.

Mississippi

THE NAME

Mississippi is the French spelling of a Chippewa word, *mici-zibi*, which means "large river." Robert de La Salle, the famous French explorer, told the world of the Mississippi River after he successfully navigated it to its mouth in 1682.

SPOTLIGHT ON HISTORY

De Soto, Marquette, Jolliet, and La Salle were some of the explorers who entered this Louisiana territory inhabited by the Chickasaws, the Choctaws, and the Natchez Indians.

Early in the 1700's French companies began sending men to Mississippi to establish colonies there. Women were later recruited as wives for these lonely settlers. The colonization efforts, however, were short-lived, because Britain took over the territory—which was then part of Florida—as a result of her victory in the Seven Years' War.

In the midst of dissenting land claims by England, France, Spain, and Georgia, Mississippi was made a territory in 1798. Her continuing conflict with Indian tribes was finally settled with their decisive defeat by Andrew Jackson's forces at the Battle of Horseshoe Bend, March 27, 1814.

IMPORTANT DATES

1540-41—Hernando de Soto explores the area.

1673—Marquette and Jolliet navigate the Mississippi River as far as the mouth of the Arkansas.

1682—La Salle claims Louisiana territory for France.

1699—French settlement begins.

1763—Britain takes possession of the area as part of West Florida.

1783—Britain cedes land to the United States at the end of the Revolution.

1795—Treaty of Lorenzo is signed, in which Spain acknowledges American sovereignty over region.

1798—Mississippi becomes a territory.

1814—Andrew Jackson routs Indians at Horseshoe Bend.

1817—Mississippi becomes the twentieth state.

Missouri

THE NAME

The Missouris were a small Algonkian tribe, and they lived at the mouth of the river that came to bear their name. The Jesuit missionary and explorer Jacques Marquette recorded their name on his map in 1673 as *8emess8rit* (the number "8" was used for the French "ou"). He learned that the word *missouri* meant "canoe haver," a reference to the dugout canoes that this Indian tribe used on the river.

Missouri later became known as the Show Me State. This evolved, according to local stories, in the late 1890's, when railroad conductors required *each* individual on trainloads of free government riders to "show me your ticket."

SPOTLIGHT ON HISTORY

Missouri, whose borders are touched by eight other states, had a rocky birth. In 1820 the territory was the subject of a fierce Congressional battle that ended in the compromise acceptance of Missouri as a potential slave state, Maine as a free state, and all territory above Missouri's southern border closed to slavery. When the Civil War erupted forty years later, Missouri stayed in the Union, and contributed 109,000 men to fight on President Lincoln's side. However, at least 30,000 Missourians also volunteered to serve in the Confederate forces.

IMPORTANT DATES
1682—La Salle claims Louisiana territory.
1735—First permanent settlement is made at Ste. Genevieve.
1762—France cedes land to Spain.
1802—Spain returns it to France.
1803—President Jefferson buys entire Louisiana territory.
1820—Congressional compromise prepares way for statehood.
1821—Missouri becomes the twenty-fourth state.
1861—Missouri sides with the Union in the Civil War.

Montana

THE NAME

The name *Montana*, Spanish for "mountainous," was unsuccessfully proposed by Congressman James M. Ashley of Ohio for a territory that was given the name *Idaho*. Ashley, a powerful member of the House Committee on Territories, however, liked the name and continued to insist that it be used for an American territory. It was accepted the next year, 1864, for the Territory of Montana. This was an apt description for an area that was 40 percent mountains and included the Continental Divide.

SPOTLIGHT ON HISTORY

After Lewis and Clark had thoroughly explored this area between 1804 and 1806, fur traders and missionaries tried their hands. Following the discovery of gold in the 1850's, boom towns sprang up, filled by prospectors and settlers. The communities of Virginia City and Helena became part of the American frontier scene. Conditions were rough in this undeveloped land where there was little law and plenty of disorder. This was changed somewhat when vigilante groups showed the numerous road agents a form of justice that their necks couldn't tolerate.

With one frontier problem resolved, another one arose in the late 1860's—renewed Indian fighting. The most famous incident of this type occurred not far from Hardin, Montana, on June 25, 1876, when George Armstrong Custer and his troops were killed at the Battle of the Little Bighorn.

The time finally came in 1889 for Montana to join the Union as an equal among the other forty states.

IMPORTANT DATES
1742—François and Louis de La Vérendrye crossed southwest Montana.
1804—Lewis and Clark explore region.
1850's—Gold rush begins.
1864—Montana Territory is formed from eastern Idaho.
1876—Custer defeated at the Battle of Little Bighorn.
1877—Chief Joseph, Nez Percé leader, surrenders.
1889—Montana becomes the forty-first state.

Nebraska

THE NAME

The Sioux tribal name for the main river in this area was *Niboapka*, "broad or flat water." The French similarly called this river, which spread out widely along its course, *la Rivière Platte*, "the broad river." In later years, John C. Fremont, the American general and explorer, suggested that Congress accept the Indian name for the new territory.

SPOTLIGHT ON HISTORY

The development of this part of America followed the same basic pattern of other frontier regions—early Spanish and French exploration, charting of the area by Lewis and Clark, the establishment of fur-trading settlements, and the migration of farmers and townspeople.

The 1854 Kansas–Nebraska Act opened this new territory to land-hungry settlers who were given the right to decide the question of slavery locally. However, rapid settlement only began with the Homestead Act of 1862, which permitted homesteaders to claim 160 acres of free land.

Nebraska was once a land of many Indians—40,000 in eight tribes. Today, there are 14,000 on three reservations.

IMPORTANT DATES
1541—Francisco de Coronado explores area.
1803—The United States purchases Louisiana Territory.
1804—Lewis and Clark explore area.
1854—Kansas–Nebraska Act divides territory in two.
1862—Homestead Act gives free land to settlers.
1867—Nebraska is admitted as the thirty-seventh state.

Nevada

THE NAME

Spanish explorers, sailing near the coast of California, saw high snow-capped mountains which they called *sierra nevada*, "snowy range." In the early 1860's, a territorial convention decided on *Nevada* after considering such names as Washoe, and Esmeralda. The region was once called the Washoe Territory, having taken the name of famous silver diggings situated near the Washoe Indian tribe.

SPOTLIGHT ON HISTORY

Exploration began late in Nevada with such frontiersmen as Jedediah Smith and John C. Frémont exploring and charting the region in the second quarter of the 1800's. The United States acquired the land, shortly thereafter, as a result of the Mexican War. Soon the region, part of the Utah Territory, became a scene of mass migration, with thousands entering to get their shares of the famous gold and silver strike, the Comstock Lode.

Nevada then grew fast, attaining territorial status in 1861. Statehood came rapidly three years later because President Abraham Lincoln was anxious to have the support of another free state in the Civil War.

IMPORTANT DATES

1826—Jedediah Smith, fur trader and explorer, crosses Nevada.

1843—John C. Frémont begins scientific expeditions here.

1848—Treaty of Guadalupe-Hidalgo is signed, ending Mexican War and ceding Nevada region to the United States.

1859—Comstock Lode is discovered.

1861—Nevada Territory is created.

1864—Nevada becomes the thirty-sixth state.

New Hampshire

THE NAME

John Mason, a resident of the English county of Hampshire, was given a deed to land in America that he called New Hampshire. He died six years later, in 1635, without ever having seen his vast holdings.

SPOTLIGHT ON HISTORY

The heirs of John Mason had a very difficult time proving full title to their land. Court battles went on for 150 years after his death. In addition, New Hampshire had boundary disputes with her neighbors, Massachusetts and New York. After New Hampshire dissolved its earlier ties with Massachusetts in 1679, it flourished on its own.

Residents of the Granite State did their share in America's earlier wars. They may well have been the first participants in the Revolution by virtue of their 1774 capture of Fort William and Mary at Portsmouth Harbor. In the War of 1812, they drafted 35,000 men in addition to volunteering a fleet of privateers. And they felt the full impact of the Civil War, losing almost 10 percent of their 38,000 Federal soldiers.

New Hampshire had the honor of being the ninth, and decisive, state to ratify the new United States Constitution.

IMPORTANT DATES
1623 — Permanent settlements are made at Portsmouth and Dover.
1641 — New Hampshire becomes part of Massachusetts.
1679 — New Hampshire becomes a separate royal province.
1788 — On June 21, New Hampshire ratifies the Constitution, thus establishing its authority, and becomes the ninth state.

New Jersey

THE NAME

Two English noblemen were granted this tract of land by James, Duke of York (afterward King James II). One of the grantees, Sir George Carteret, named the area New Jersey in honor of the Channel Island of Jersey, where he was born.

SPOTLIGHT ON HISTORY

In 1524 Giovanni da Verrazano sailed his French ship along this Atlantic coastline, although he missed both Chesapeake and Delaware bays. Eighty-five years later Henry Hudson delved deeper into the region, an important step for the future settlement of the Dutch colony of New Netherland. In 1664 it fell to an English fleet under the ultimate command of the Lord High Admiral, the Duke of York.

New Jersey and New York have had closely knit histories, with the governor of the latter once serving as the chief administrator of both colonies in the early 1770's. Howver, by the time of the American Revolution, New Jersey was on its own, participating in the war independently. Almost one hundred skirmishes took place in the Garden State, the most important being the battles of Trenton, Princeton, and Monmouth.

IMPORTANT DATES
1524 — Verrazano explores New Jersey's coast.
1609 — Hudson sails up what was to become the Hudson River.
1660 — Dutch settle at Bergen.
1664 — English capture New Amsterdam and take control of New Jersey.
1776 — Washington crosses the Delaware to defeat the Hessians at Trenton.
1787 — December 19, New Jersey becomes the third state to ratify the Constitution.

New Mexico

THE NAME

This land, in the upper Rio Grande region, was called Nuevo Méjico as early as 1591. Spanish explorers hoped that it would provide the same riches as Mexico did.

SPOTLIGHT ON HISTORY

But there proved to be no gold-filled rooms in this namesake of Old Mexico. The Spaniards, however, did take advantage of the rich land by colonizing the area.

Throughout the many years of Spanish rule and missionary work, an intermingling of Hispanic, Indian, and Anglo-American cultures evolved. This can be seen in all walks of life throughout New Mexico. Forty percent of the population here is Spanish-American, the highest in the nation.

However, not all the Indians took kindly to the Spaniard's religion and customs. The Navajos and Apaches were a constant threat to their conquerors, because they would not accept their life-styles. They offered similar resistance to their new conquerors, the Americans, who herded them into reservations. The Apaches revolted in the 1870's and 1880's, fighting for what they would never regain. Their battle for independence and dignity came to an end in 1886 when Geronimo surrendered.

IMPORTANT DATES
1540 — Francisco de Coronado explores area.

1680—Pueblo Indians drive Spaniards back to Mexico.
1690's—Spanish reconquer land.
1821—Mexico wins independence from Spain.
1848—New Mexico becomes part of the United States after the Mexican War.
1886—Geronimo surrenders.
1912—New Mexico becomes the forty-seventh state.

New York

THE NAME

New York was named in honor of James, Duke of York, after his forces captured New Amsterdam, the capital of the Dutch colony of New Netherland. This younger brother of Charles II was granted title to all the land between the Connecticut River and Delaware Bay.

SPOTLIGHT ON HISTORY

In 1626, acting for the Dutch West India Company, Peter Minuit bought Manhattan Island from the local Indians for a trunkload of trinkets worth sixty guilders (twenty-four dollars). This real-estate transaction took place almost a century after Giovanni da Verrazano had first sailed his French ship into New York Bay and seventeen years after Henry Hudson had explored the region.

The colonies that the Dutch established were captured and occupied by the English in 1664. New York was the last colony (except for the belatedly founded Georgia) to be granted a legislative assembly; it was 1691 before the first assembly met.

The strategically placed colony was directly involved in almost every European war that lapped over into America—King William's War, Queen Anne's War, King George's War, and the Seven Year's War (the French and Indian War).

IMPORTANT DATES
1524—Verrazano sails into New York Bay.
1609—Henry Hudson sails into the region for the Dutch, navigating the river that later would bear his name.

1614—Dutch built Fort Nassau at what is now Albany, thus making this the second-oldest European city in the United States.

1626—Peter Minuit buys Manhattan for the Dutch.

1664—New Amsterdam is captured by the English and renamed New York.

1788—June 26, New York ratifies the Constitution and becomes the eleventh state.

1789—President George Washington is inaugurated in New York City, the nation's first capital.

Ohio

THE NAME

The Iroquois called this river *Ohiiyo*, which in the Seneca language means "beautiful" or "magnificent." In 1680 the French explorer Robert de La Salle made note of this *belle rivière*, giving it the spelling that it has today. The territory took its name from the river, and the state took it from the territory.

According to local accounts, Ohio gots its nickname, "the Buckeye State," in the early days of its territorial status. At this time Ohio Indians gave the name *Hetuch*, meaning the large eyes of the buck deer, to the area's first administrator, a very big, imposing man. He became known, thereafter, as Big Buckeye.

SPOTLIGHT ON HISTORY

The settling of Ohio proved to be a very painful process, with border disputes and Indian uprisings going on almost up to the state's admittance into the Union. The Miami, Shawnee, and Wyandot tribes, who were eighteenth-century emigrants to Ohio, were reluctant to share the land with the white man. During the Revolution they, together with Tories and Canadians, engaged in fierce fighting with American soldiers. Their uprisings were permanently ended in 1794, when General Anthony Wayne defeated a large Indian force at the Battle of Fallen Timbers.

IMPORTANT DATES

1669—Louis Jolliet explores area.

1679–80—Robert de La Salle travels down the Ohio River.

1754–63—French and Indian War rages.

1763-64—Indian rising led by Chief Pontiac breaks out across the frontier.
1777-83—American Revolution flames in the west, bringing Indian attacks.
1794—General Anthony Wayne defeats the tribes at Fallen Timbers.
1803—Ohio becomes the seventeenth state.

Oklahoma

THE NAME

In the Choctaw Indian language, *oklahoma* is a combination of two words meaning "red people." In 1866, the Reverend Allen Wright, a Choctaw chief and missionary, suggested that this name be used for the area which was then known as the Indian Territory. Oklahoma received its name accordingly—and appropriately, for a large number of America's Indians still live there.

Oklahoma got its nickname "the Sooner State" from the Sooners—persons who occupied lands in the Indian Territory before it was officially opened. On April 22, 1889, fifty thousand homesteaders anxiously waited on the boundary line, ready to rush in at the designated hour to stake their claims. However, when they crossed the line, they found many people had gotten to the new land "sooner" than they were supposed to.

SPOTLIGHT ON HISTORY

As a result of the 1830 Indian Removal Act, thousands of Indians from the Five Civilized Tribes (Chickasaw, Cherokee, Choctaw, Creek, and Seminole) were relocated in Oklahoma. The worst of these forced moves, one of the most disgraceful episodes in American history, ultimately became known as the Trail of Tears, for the hardship and suffering of the Cherokee removees.

The official Oklahoma state seal honors these tribes with a five-pointed star, each point showing a symbol representing one particular tribe.

IMPORTANT DATES
1803—Oklahoma is purchased as part of Louisiana Territory.
1830—The Indian Removal Act sends many tribes here from eastern parts of the United States.
1838—The Cherokee follow the Trail of Tears, long forced march to Oklahoma.

1889—Land is opened for settlement.
1907—Oklahoma becomes the forty-sixth state.

Oregon

THE NAME

This name probably came from the French word *ouragan*, "hurricane." Explorers thought that the Columbia River, described as "the river of the squalls," would lead to the fabled Northwest Passage to the Orient.

The Oregon River—the poet's name for the Columbia—was made famous by William Cullen Bryant in his poen *"Thanatopsis."*

SPOTLIGHT ON HISTORY

This northwest part of the United States was another area that Meriwether Lewis and William Clark explored for forthcoming generations of Americans. They journeyed, in 1804, from St. Louis to the mouth of the Columbia River.

Twenty years later, fur traders and missionaries moved into the region, fulfilling another step in the settlement process. Then, in 1843, a large number of American settlers, over a thousand, came to Oregon over the famed Oregon trail, to clear the forests and start new lives.

IMPORTANT DATES
1792—Columbia River is discovered by an American sea captain, Robert
      Gray.
1804-1806—Lewis and Clark explore the Columbia.
1834—Settlement begins.
1843—Twelve hundred immigrants arrive by way of the Oregon Trail.
1848—Oregon is formed into a territory.
1859—Oregon becomes the thirty-third state.

Pennsylvania

THE NAME

On January 5, 1681, William Penn wrote a letter to a friend telling him about the land charter that he had received from Charles II:

Know that after many waitings, watchings, soliciting and disputes in council, this day my country confirmed to me under the great seal of England, with large powers and privileges, by the name of Pennsilvania, a name the king would give in honour of my father . . . though I much opposed it, and went to the king to have it struck out and altered, he said 'twas past . . . nor could twenty guineas move the undersecretarys to vary the name . . . .

Thus the new colony was given the name "Penn's Woods."

SPOTLIGHT ON HISTORY

William Penn wanted a colony in the New World where people of good will could live together in peace. This was his hope for the community that he and other Quakers settled, and whose capital they named Philadelphia, a Greek term meaning "brotherly love."

This land, which had previously been the subject of great rivalry between Sweden and Holland, came into the hands of the British in 1664. Two decades later, Penn and his followers took control of it. They worked hard to achieve their goal, and in time Penn's "Holy Experiment" proved successful. Pennsylvania grew prosperous, doing well in its farming and other industries.

So tolerant were Pennsylvanians that exotic religious groups all over central Europe packed up their membership and moved to America en masse. Many such small sects still survive. In time Philadelphia became the largest city in the colonies and the most sophisticated.

IMPORTANT DATES

1609—Henry Hudson sails into Delaware Bay.

1638—Swedish settlement is established on the Delaware.

1655—Peter Stuyvesant, governor of New Netherland, captures the Swedish colony and establishes Dutch rule.

1664—English seize Dutch territories.

1681—William Penn receives charter from Charles II.

1774—On September 5, First Continental Congress assembles at Carpenter's Hall, adjourns October 26.

1775—On May 10, Second Continental Congress assembles in the State House, adjourns December 20, 1776.

1776—On July 2, independence is voted; two days later, John Hancock, president of the Congress, signs the Declaration.

1787—The Constitutional Convention sits in Philadelphia, May 25 to September 17; on December 12, Pennsylvania ratifies the Constitution, the second state to do so.

1790-1800—Philadelphia serves as the nation's second capital.

Rhode Island

THE NAME

The name Rhode Island may have come from several different sources. The land was described by Verrazano as "about the bigness of the Island of Rhodes"—a Greek island in the Mediterranean Sea. (In Greek, the name means "roses.") However, in the early 1600's Dutch sea captain Adriaen Block noted "the fiery aspect of the place, caused by the red clay in some portions of its shores." His Dutch name for it was "Roodt Eylandt" (Red Island).

This is the smallest state with the largest name—State of Rhode Island and Providence Plantations.

SPOTLIGHT ON HISTORY

Rhode Island is famous as the haven that Roger Williams fled to in 1636 after he was banished from Massachusetts for religious and other reasons. He and his followers were determined to make their newfound home a place of religious refuge and freedom. Pursuing this goal, Rhode Islanders got a royal charter from King Charles II in 1663, which gave them the right to "hold forth a lively experiment that a most flourishing civil state may stand and best be maintained with full liberty in religious concernments."

As indicated here, Rhode Island has kept its promises:

1638—First Baptist congregation in United States.

1699—Oldest Quaker meetinghouse in nation.

1763—Oldest Jewish synagogue (building) in America—Touro Synagogue.

OTHER IMPORTANT DATES

1524—Verrazano sails into the area, discovers Narragansett Bay.

1636—Roger Williams settles Providence.

1663—Charles II grants charter.

1790—On May 29, Rhode Island ratifies the Constitution of the United
States, the last of the original thirteen colonies to do so, and becomes
the thirteenth state.

Tennessee

THE NAME

"Tennessee' is derived from *Tanasi*, a Cherokee name for two Indian
villages that existed in this area. The name was later used for a nearby
stream, then for the river it flowed into, and finally for the land that the river
went through.

SPOTLIGHT ON HISTORY

Tennessee's early history followed a pattern similar to several other
states in this region: sixteenth-century Spanish exploration, further exploratory journeys in the seventeenth century by the Frenchmen Marquette, Jolliet, and La Salle, finally American occupation and settlement.

The people of Tennessee readily participated in several American wars.
They earned the nickname, "the Volunteer State," by their willingness to
join the ranks during the Mexican War. In the Civil War, they had more
troops in the Confederate Army than any other Southern state—115,000.
East Tennessee, however, was opposed to secession and remained in the
Union. They sent 30,000 young men to fight on the side of the North.

IMPORTANT DATES
1540—Hernando de Soto explores the area.
1673—Marquette and Jolliet canoe down the Mississippi.
1682—La Salle and others build a fort at the mouth of the Hatchie River.
1769—Settlers from Virginia set up the first permanent white community.
1796—Tennessee is admitted as the sixteenth state.

Texas

THE NAME

In this area, more than four hundred years ago, the Caddo Indians called tribes that they had good relations with *teysha*, "friends." The conquering Spanish gave this name to all the tribes of the Caddo Confederacy. In time, the entire region became known as "the land of the Texas Indians."

SPOTLIGHT ON HISTORY

There was a large time gap between Spain's exploration, 1519, and settlement, 1682, of Texas. But once colonization began, Spain maintained a long rule over this section of the New World. Her reign finally crumbled with Mexico's independence in 1821, which was accompanied by an avowal of Texas loyalty to the new republic.

Many Americans settled in Texas in the 1820's and 1830's, and when Antonio López de Santa Anna proclaimed himself dictator of Mexico, they broke away and formed their own republic. Besieged and wiped out at an abandoned San Antonio mission called the Alamo (Spanish for "poplar tree"), Texans rallied under Sam Houston and soon reversed this disaster with a decisive victory over Santa Anna at San Jacinto, near Houston, March 2, 1836.

Thereupon, the Lone Star State joined the nations of the world as a sovereign country. Texas was admitted to the Union in 1845, an event that triggered the Mexican War.

IMPORTANT DATES

1519—Area is claimed for Spain by Alonso de Pineda.
1541—Vasquez de Coronado explores parts of Texas.
1682—First permanent Spanish settlement is made at El Paso.
1685—La Salle builds a fort for the French.
1821—Mexico gains independence from Spain.
1835—Texans revolt against Santa Anna.
1836—Texas becomes an independent nation.
1845—Texas is annexed to the United States as the twenty-eighty state.

Utah

THE NAME

This region was named for the Ute (or Utah) Indians who, as their name signifies in the Apache language, lived "higher up" in the mountains than the other tribes.

The Mormons, early settlers of this land, called it "Deseret" (from a Mormon word meaning "honeybee"), a name that Congress turned down.

SPOTLIGHT ON HISTORY

The history of the Mormons—officially, the Church of Jesus Christ of Latter-Day Saints—and of Utah cross in 1847, the year when this religious group moved there. From their founding in 1830 to their Utah settlement in 1847, the Mormons had tried to establish a permanent community in several other states. Hostile neighbors pushed them out of New York, Ohio, Missouri, and Illinois. Their leader, Joseph Smith, was killed in Nauvoo, Illinois. Following this mistreatment, they migrated to the area now known as Utah, establishing the Provisional State of Deseret. This large territory at that time encompassed all of Utah and Nevada, and parts of Oregon, Idaho, Wyoming, Colorado, New Mexico, Arizona, and California. As soon as the Mormons were established, they petitioned Congress for admission as a state. The legislature denied them statehood, but did allow territorial status for an area much smaller than the original region.

Utah eventually became a state, having survived many years of conflict between Mormons and non-Mormons, and after struggling against Federal laws that attempted to regulate the social and economic lives of the Mormon people.

IMPORTANT DATES
1776—Spanish explorers visit Utah.
1847—Mormons settle Salt Lake City.
1848—The United States acquires area from Mexico.
1849—Mormons organize State of Deseret.
1850—Territory of Utah is created by Congress.
1896—Utah becomes the forty-fifth state.

Vermont

THE NAME

An outstanding geographic feature of Vermont is its green mountains, or *verts monts* as written in slightly incorrect French. The mountain range was noticed by the French explorer Samuel de Champlain in 1609, a century and a half before Dr. Thomas Young of Philadelphia suggested that Congress accept the name *Vermont*. The region had previously been known as New Connecticut.

SPOTLIGHT ON HISTORY

Vermont was not well settled until after the French and Indian War. Then, as newcomers arrived, they were caught between New York and New Hampshire claims to the region. Ethan Allen's rugged Green Mountain Boys were originally formed to fight the "enemy" from New York.

But Vermont men were strong opponents of the English in the two wars America had with them. The Green Mountain Boys first seized Fort Ticonderoga from its unwary British garrison, then joined forces with New Hampshire men to battle invading John Burgoyne. And in the War of 1812, America's Second War of Independence, Vermont ships prevented Great Britain from occupying the strategic area between New England and New York.

IMPORTANT DATES

1609—Samuel de Champlain explores the area.

1724—Fort Dummer, first permanent settlement, is erected near modern Brattleboro.

1777—Vermont declares itself an independent republic.

1791—Vermont enters the Union as the fourteenth state, the first one to be admitted after the original thirteen.

Virginia

THE NAME

Virginia, the first English colony in America, was named for the unmarried Queen Elizabeth I. Elizabeth was known throughout her forty-five-year reign as the Virgin Queen.

SPOTLIGHT ON HISTORY

Virginia grew from a struggling settlement in Jamestown to become a leader of the thirteen colonies. It was a Virginian, Richard Henry Lee, who proposed the independence resolution to the Second Continental Congress.

Geographically, seven states or parts of states were carved out of the vast Virginia territory that James I granted to the Virginia Company of London in 1609—Ohio, Illinois, Indiana, Michigan, Wisconsin, West Virginia, and Kentucky.

Politically, this southern state was the mother of Presidents, having sent four men to the highest office in America during the early years of the republic: George Washington, Thomas Jefferson, James Madison, and James Monroe. Presidents William Henry Harrison, John Tyler, Zachary Taylor, and Woodrow Wilson were born in Virginia but were residents of other states when elected.

Her leadership continued throughout the nineteenth century, and Virginians played important roles in the states' rights struggle before, during, and after the Civil War.

IMPORTANT DATES

1584—Elizabeth I names the region Virginia.

1607—Jamestown is settled, the first permanent English enclave in the New World.

1624—Virginia becomes a royal colony.

1776—Virginia proposes independence.

1788—On June 25, Virginia ratifies the Constitution, becoming the tenth state.

1861—Virginia secedes from the Union; the capital of the Confederacy is moved from Montgomery, Alabama, to Richmond.

Washington

THE NAME

This land, in the northwest corner of America, was first named by a British sea captain in 1792. He called it New Georgia in honor of King George III of England. After the United States acquired the territory from Britain, it was called Columbia, then changed to Washington in honor of the first President.

It is an interesting coincidence in history that the territory bore the names of the two opposing leaders of the American Revolution—George Washington and George III.

SPOTLIGHT ON HISTORY

In the early 1800's this remote region, bordering on Canada and the Pacific Ocean, was an important fur-trapping area. The lucrative business opportunities were recognized by John Jacob Astor, who set up fur-trading posts in 1811 and 1812.

Soon the missionaries and their families came, opening the territory for the future flow of permanent settlers. This settlement was hastened with the signing of the Oregon Treaty, a pact that ended boundary disputes between the United States and Great Britain. The agreement gave Britain ownership of all territory above the 49th parallel, with the United States taking legal possession of the land below this geographical line. Soon after, the area was split into the territories of Oregon and Washington.

IMPORTANT DATES

1775—Bruno Heceta discovers the mouth of Columbia River, claims part of region for Spain.

1811—Fort Okanogan, first American settlement, is made by fur traders.

1836—Marcus Whitman, a missionary, establishes permanent settlement at Walla-Walla.

1846—Oregon Treaty resolves American and English land dispute.

1848—Oregon Territory is created.

1853—Washington Territory is created.

1889—Washington is admitted into the Union as the forty-second state.

West Virginia

THE NAME

This former part of Virginia bears the same name as the first English colony, a name given by Elizabeth I, the Virgin Queen of England.

When West Virginia was carved out of its mother state during the Civil War, it was suggested, at a state convention, that it be given a different name. Harmon Sinsel, an influential delegate, rose to speak against the notion: "I was born and raised in Virginia and I have ever been proud of that name. I admit that Virginians have been wrong and that many of them in this rebellion have disgraced themselves; but that has not weaned me from the name. . . ."

The vote was then taken for the following names:
West Virginia—30
Kanawha—9
Western Virginia—2
Augusta—1

SPOTLIGHT ON HISTORY

The people who lived in the eastern and western parts of Virginia were quite different from each other. Many western Virginians, for example, had emigrated from Pennsylvania, Maryland, and New York, and had little use for slaves. Unlike their brethren in the eastern part of the state, they were not highly educated, had little money, and did not belong to the cultured Episcopal Church, as did so many Virginians. Moreover, they had little contact with the eastern Virginians, for it took a week to travel from the mountains to Richmond. In addition, the eastern Virginians, in control of state affairs, often discriminated against the mountain people—socially, economically, and politically.

Thus, when Virginia seceded from the Union, the counties of the west similarly voted to secede from Virginia and remain with the North.

IMPORTANT DATES
1861—April 17, Virginia secedes from the Union.
June 11, counties of western Virginia declare Virginia's secession illegal.
August 20, new state of Kanawha is created by western Virginians.
November 26, name is changed to West Virginia.
1862—April 3, West Virginian constitution is accepted by Congress.
1863—April 20, President Lincoln signs proclamation admitting West Virginia to the Union.
June 20, West Virginia officially becomes the thirty-fifth state.

Wisconsin

THE NAME

Glaciers had dug out large depressions in this area, which were eventually filled in by thousands of lakes. This natural phenomenon caused the Chippewa Indians to name their land *Meskousing*—"where the waters gather." French explorers called the main river in the region *Ouisconsin*, apparently their own spelling of the Chippewa word. This was finally Americanized to Wisconsin.

Wisconsin got the nickname, "the Badger State," during the mining boom of the 1820's. At that time, because of the shortage in housing, lead miners lived in hillside caves and abandoned mine shafts, and were thus called badgers.

SPOTLIGHT ON HISTORY

France claimed this area in 1672, sending in the explorers Marquette and Jolliet one year later to chart it in detail. Almost a century later, at the end of the French and Indian War, France was forced to cede this fur-rich region to Great Britain.

In 1783 the land was officially ceded to the United States. However, it took another thirty years, and another war—the War of 1812—to get England completely out of the territory.

IMPORTANT DATES

1634—Jean Nicolet visits area to arrange French fur-trading agreements with the Indians.

1672—French claim region.

1673—Marquette and Jolliet explore territory.

1763—British take possession of region.

1783—Land ceded to the United States.

1836—Territory of Wisconsin is formed.

1848—Wisconsin becomes the thirtieth state.

Wyoming

THE NAME

The name "Wyoming" was derived from two Delaware Indian words, *meche-weamiing*, meaning "at the big flats." It was an eastern Indian word that was interpreted by whites to mean "the large plains"—a fitting description for the western territory called Wyoming.

There is a town named Wyoming in Pennsylvania and a Wyoming County in New York.

SPOTLIGHT ON HISTORY

After the explorers, the missionaries, and the beaver-pelt hunters came the lusty men and women settlers. They traveled, in the 1840's, over the Oregon Trail with their horses, oxen, and wagons, seeking farms and homesteads. Women were recognized as warranting a very important, and, in many ways, an equal place in this frontier territory. Perhaps this is why "the Equality State" set aside a special day, December 10, to commemorate the anniversary of women's right to vote in Wyoming.

WYOMING AND WOMEN'S RIGHTS

1870—First woman to be appointed a justice of the peace (Esther Morris, "Mother of Women Suffrage" in Wyoming).

1889—Female suffrage bill signed.

1910—First woman elected to Wyoming legislature (Mary Bellamy).

1911—First woman in Wyoming elected to office of mayor (Susan Wissler).

1924—First woman elected to office of governor in the United States (Nellie Ross).

OTHER IMPORTANT DATES

1807-08—White man, John Colter, explores Wyoming.

1868—Wyoming Territory is created.

1890—Wyoming becomes the forty-fourth state.

District of Columbia

President George Washington chose an area around the Potomac River to be the permanent capital of the United States. Land for the city of Washington, located in the District of Columbia, was donated by the surrounding states of Maryland and Virginia. Virginia's half was later returned to her.

The city and the district, both situated on the same sixty-nine square miles, were named in honor of men who played roles in the formation and development of America—Christopher Columbus and George Washington.

By the year 1800, the city was ready, though not completed, for President John Adams to move in, making it the third capital of the United States.

Virgin Islands

As Columbus sailed through these waters on his second New World voyage in 1493, he sighted many small islands. They reminded him, it is said, of a third-century saint, Ursula, who was supposedly martyred by the Huns along with eleven thousand other virgin nuns.

Panama Canal Zone

The Panama Canal Zone is a strip of land ten miles wide and fifty-one miles long. The United States leases it from the country of Panama. A canal was opened here in 1914 connecting the Atlantic and Pacific Oceans for oceangoing vessels. Prior to this, ships heading for the Pacific had to travel thousands of miles around the tip of South America.

Puerto Rico

THE NAME

Christopher Columbus came upon this island during his second voyage across the Atlantic. He called it San Juan Bautista ("Saint John the Baptist"), a name that was later changed to Porto Rico ("rich port") to signify a place that the gold-laden Spanish ships stopped at on their way from Mexico to Spain. The spelling was officially changed to its correct Spanish form in 1932.

SPOTLIGHT ON HISTORY

In 1508 King Ferdinand of Spain sent Juan Ponce de Leon to occupy this Caribbean island. The famous conquistador, accompanied by a small force of soldiers, easily overcame the native Indians. Spain then proceeded with the colonization of Puerto Rico, managing to maintain tight control over her rich port for the next four centuries despite English and Dutch attacks.

During these years the island became, in many ways, a reflection of Spain, with the people adopting the Spanish language, religion, and culture.

The Spanish reign over Puerto Rico ended in 1898, when Spain was defeated by the United States in the Spanish-American War, and Puerto Rico became an American territory.

IMPORTANT DATES

1493—Columbus claims island for Spain.

1508—Ponce de Leon conquers the island people in preparation for Spanish colonization.

1897—People of Puerto Rico win greater self-government from Spain.

1898—Spanish cede island to the United States at the end of the Spanish-American War.

1952—Puerto Rico votes for commonwealth status in the United States.

 **3**

NAMES OF PRESIDENTS

Most of the individuals who have won what is considered the most prestigious public position in the world—the United States presidency—have had the additional tribute of having places named for them.

Every imaginable type of locale bears the name of a Chief Executive—and for a variety of reasons. The President may have just been elected or inaugurated, visited the region, or helped the people in the area. Compassion may have been fired up by his recent death in office. He may have been a native son or may have moved to the area or died there.

Some places were named for the men long before they ran for the presidency, while they held a different position, civilian or military, in public life.

Most names are found nationwide, but some sections of the country favor certain Presidents and avoid others. In the South, for example, very few places bear the name "Lincoln."

The earlier Presidents dominate the list of names, for obvious reasons. The country was developing in their day, and there were many new places to name. And the more popular a President was, the more towns took his name. Someimtes, in our pioneering, mobile society, a name was transferred from one location to another.

Normally, it's the man's last name that is used. But a number of towns—Quincy, Stonewall, Ulysses, Woodrow—carry first names or sobriquets.

Most of the places cited in this chapter, but not necessarily all of them, are named for Presidents. Occasionally the name is a coincidence.

GEORGE WASHINGTON, FIRST PRESIDENT
1789-1797

There are towns named Washington in Alabama, Arkansas, Colorado, Florida, Georgia, Idaho, Illinois, Indiana, Iowa, Kansas, Kentucky, Louisiana, Maine, Maryland, Minnesota, Mississippi, Missouri, Nebraska, New York, North Carolina, Ohio, Oklahoma, Oregon, Pennsylvania, Rhode Island, Tennessee, Texas, Utah, Vermont, Virginia, and Wisconsin. There is also a Washingtonville, Ohio.

More than seventy places in the United States bear the name Washington—the most places named for any individual. A state (the only state that bears the name of a man), the nation's capital, cities, towns, mountains, lakes, rivers, crossings, depots, groves, parks, terraces, and valleys have been named after the first President. The naming has been widespread, covering all regions of the country. A mountain has even been named in honor of his wife Martha—Mount Lady Washington in Colorado.

Fort Washington, New York (1776), was the first in a long line of namings.

Washington, Virginia, was surveyed by Washington himself.

In the early 1770's, the Crown gave land grants to setlers who migrated to what is now Washington, Georgia. Many of them were Virginians from Westmoreland County, birthplace of George Washington. The town was incorporated as Washington on January 23, 1780. In Georgia today it is called Washington-Wilkes (Wilkes is the county of which Washington is the seat) to distinguish it from Washington, D.C.

Several noteworthy *firsts* occurred in or near this handsome little Georgia city:

- Eli Whitney perfected and set up the first successful cotton gin in 1793 at the Mount Pleasant Plantation, seven miles west of here.
- In 1804 Sarah Hillhouse became the first woman newspaper editor in the United States. She worked for the Washington *Monitor*.

And a significant *last*:

- President Jefferson Davis conducted the last meeting of the Confederate Cabinet here on May 5, 1865, signing the last Confederate state papers and officially dissolving the government. Five days later, a hundred miles south of Washington-Wilkes in Irwinville, Davis was taken prisoner by Federal troops.

Formerly called Liverpool, the town of Washington, Indiana, took on its thoroughly American name in 1817, soon after America's second War of Independence with Great Britain.

JOHN ADAMS, SECOND PRESIDENT
1797-1801

There are towns named Adams in Colorado, Idaho, Illinois, Indiana, Iowa, Mississippi, Nebraska, North Carolina, Ohio, Pennsylvania, Tennessee, Texas, Utah, Washington, and Wisconsin. There is also an Adamsville, Alabama.

THOMAS JEFFERSON, THIRD PRESIDENT
1801-1809

There are towns named Jefferson in Alabama, Arkansas, Colorado, Florida, Georgia, Idaho, Illinois, Indiana, Iowa, Kansas, Kentucky, Louisiana, Mississippi, Missouri, Montana, Nebraska, New York, Ohio, Oklahoma, Oregon, Pennsylvania, Tennessee, Texas, Washington, West Virginia, and Wisconsin. There is a Jeffersonville in Indiana, Kentucky, and Ohio.

The town of Dartmouth, New Hampshire, changed its name to Jefferson on December 8, 1796, one month after Thomas Jefferson was elected Vice President.

On December 3, 1821, the Missouri legislature created Jefferson City, the capital of the newly admitted state, an act that, it is said, greatly pleased the seventy-eight-year-old Sage of Monticello. Many of the new citizens who settled there during the 1820's and 1830's were from Charlottesville, Virginia, the vicinity of Jefferson's home. Many had been friends and associates of his. The town was planned and laid out by Major Elias Bancroft and Daniel M. Boone, son of the famous frontiersman.

Jefferson, Iowa, was named in 1854. It's located in Greene County, which is named in honor of Revolutionary War general Nathanael Greene.

JAMES MADISON, FOURTH PRESIDENT
1809-1817

There are towns named Madison in Alabama, Arkansas, Florida, Georgia, Idaho, Illinois, Indiana, Iowa, Kentucky, Louisiana, Mississippi, Missouri, Minnesota, Nebraska, New York, North Carolina, Ohio, Tennessee, Texas, Virginia, and Wisconsin.

Originally, Madison, New Hampshire, was part of the town of Eaton. On December 17, 1852, Eaton was divided, one half becoming the town of Madison.

There is also a Mount Madison in New Hampshire's presidential range of the White Mountains.

JAMES MONROE, FIFTH PRESIDENT
1817–1825

There are towns named Monroe in Alabama, Arkansas, Florida, Georgia, Illinois, Indiana, Iowa, Kentucky, Michigan, Mississippi, Missouri, Ohio, Pennsylvania, Tennessee, West Virginia, Wisconsin, and Wyoming. There are also Monroe City and Monrovia, Indiana; Monroe Center, Wisconsin; and Monroe Bridge, Massachusetts.

Soon after James Monroe took the presidential oath of office in March 1817, he toured a large section of United States lands, inspecting military posts and visiting the American people. In honor of the new President, who came through the Michigan Territory, the county and town of Monroe were named for him.

On May 1, 1819, the packet steamer *James Monroe* was the first ship of its kind to enter the harbor of this small Louisiana town. The occurrence was celebrated by the local inhabitants with the renaming of the town in honor of the ship and the President.

Four townships are named after Presidents in Monroeville County, Indiana—Jefferson, Madison, Jackson, and Monroe. All touch at a place that is known as Four Presidents Corner.

JOHN QUINCY ADAMS, SIXTH PRESIDENT
1825–1829

There are towns named Quincy in California, Florida, Illinois, Indiana, Kansas, Massachusetts, Michigan, Mississippi, Missouri, Ohio, Oregon, and Washington.

In 1825, shortly after John Quincy Adams was elected President, the Illinois legislature created the county of Adams, naming it in his honor. A commission then selected a nearby place for the county seat, which they called Quincy. The public square within Quincy was named John's Square.

Though spelled alike, the Illinois and Massachusetts towns are pronounced differently: Quin*s*y, Illinois, and Quin*z*y, Massachusetts.

Quincy, Massachusetts, had many abolitionists, who were part of an antislavery society that helped blacks escape from the South. The slaves would be transported by boat from Missouri to Quincy, an important junction in the Underground Railway. They would then be hidden in abolitionists' homes until they were able to continue their journey to Canada.

Quincy, Illinois, was also the site of the sixth of the famous seven debates that Abraham Lincoln and Stephen Douglas engaged in during their battle for the Senate. On that occasion, October 13, 1858, each man stated his side of the argument as follows:

LINCOLN: We think it [slavery] a wrong not confining itself merely to the persons of the States where it exists, but that it is a wrong which in its tendency, to say the least, affects the existence of the whole nation. Because we think it wrong, we propose a course of policy that shall deal with it as a wrong.

DOUGLAS: If each state will only agree to mind its own business, and let its neighbors alone . . . this republic can exist forever, divided into free and slave states, as our fathers made it and the people of each state have decided.

Douglas' stand helped him to win the election to the United States Senate, but it hurt his chances two years later whan he ran nationwide against Lincoln for the presidency.

The Illinois naming was carried to many other states. For example, a local ranch and hotel owner, H. J. Bradley, called his California site Quincy in honor of Quincy, Illinois, where he had once lived.

ANDREW JACKSON, SEVENTH PRESIDENT
1829–1837

There are towns named Jackson in Alabama, Arkansas, Colorado, Florida, Georgia, Illinois, Indiana, Iowa, Kansas, Kentucky, Louisiana, Michigan, Minnesota, Mississippi, Missouri, New Hampshire, North Carolina, Ohio, Oklahoma, Oregon, South Dakota, Tennessee, Texas, West Virginia, and Wisconsin. There are towns called Jacksonville in Alabama, Arkansas, Florida, Georgia, Illinois, Iowa, Maine, Maryland, Missouri, North Carolina, Ohio, Oregon, and Texas.

In 1792, Andrew Jackson bought 300 acres of land in what is now Old Hickory, Tennessee, to build his first home for his wife. His other famous mansion, The Hermitage, is located just three miles east of Old Hickory.

At the time Missouri entered the Union, in 1821, it was the practice to correlate the names of counties and county seats. Jackson County, Missouri, was named after Andrew Jackson, and the county seat was given his slogan, "Independence." Clay County was named after Henry Clay, and its county seat was given his slogan, "Liberty."

Jackson, Tennessee, was originally called Alexandria. A Dr. Butler—Andrew Jackson's son-in-law—is given credit for being the town's founder. General Jackson, before he became President, was a frequent visitor there, traveling from his home in Nashville.

The first settlers in Jackson, New Hampshire, originally called their town New Madbury, after the seacoast village they came from, Madbury, New Hampshire. They changed its name to Adams in 1800, for John Adams, who was President at the time. The final renaming took place in 1829, for the newly elected President, Andrew Jackson.

In 1829, Horace Blackman journeyed from Berkshire, New York, to Michigan Territory to start a settlement that was named Jackson six years later.

On July 6, 1854, a convention was held in Jackson County, Michigan, at which the participants resolved to oppose the extension of slavery and "be known as Republicans until the contest be terminated." Jackson, Michigan, thus claims to be the birthplace of the Republican party, having formed the first statewide Republican organization.

At Ripon, Wisconsin, on February 28, 1854, an anti-Nebraska mass meeting revived the name Republican.

MARTIN VAN BUREN, EIGHTH PRESIDENT
1837–1841

There are towns named Van Buren in Arkansas, Iowa, Maine, Michigan, and Tennessee.

The original name of Van Buren, Maine, was Violet Brook, in honor of the first settler in the area. During most of the first half of the nineteenth century, this section of Maine was claimed by both Canada and the United States. The region was serviced for quite a while by a priest from Saint Basil, New Brunswick.

Finally, on August 9, 1842, the border dispute was settled in the Webster-Ashburton Treaty. The land provision of the treaty gave the United States about seven twelfths of the territory. The townspeople then decided to rename their town Van Buren for his efforts in their behalf while he served as President.

WILLIAM HENRY HARRISON, NINTH PRESIDENT
1841

There are towns named Harrison in Indiana, Iowa, Kentucky, Mississippi, Missouri, Ohio, Texas, and West Virginia.

JOHN TYLER, TENTH PRESIDENT
1841-1845

There are towns named Tyler in Minnesota, Texas, and West Virginia.

Tyler, Texas, for many years a pioneer trading post, was incorporated on April 11, 1846, and named in honor of John Tyler, who had left the presidency a year earlier. Tyler, elected Vice President in 1840, succeeded William Henry Harrison, who died of pneumonia one month after he assumed office. President Tyler was instrumental in bringing about the annexation of the Republic of Texas.

JAMES K. POLK, ELEVENTH PRESIDENT
1845-1849

There are towns named Polk in Arkansas, Florida, Georgia, Iowa, Minnesota, Missouri, Nebraska, North Carolina, Oregon, Tennessee, Texas, and Wisconsin. There is also a Polksville in North Carolina.

James Polk represented the region that was later named Polk, Tennessee, when he was in Congress. He was also governor of the state. He had served seven terms in the House of Representatives and one term in the governor's mansion.

The first post office and then the town of Polksville, North Carolina, were named in honor of the incumbent President, a native son of North Carolina.

ZACHARY TAYLOR, TWELFTH PRESIDENT
1849-1850

There are towns named Taylor in Arkansas, Florida, Georgia, Iowa, Kentucky, Mississippi, Texas, West Virginia, and Wisconsin. There are also Taylor Springs, Illinois, and Taylorsville, Georgia.

MILLARD FILLMORE, THIRTEENTH PRESIDENT
1850-1853

There are towns named Fillmore in Illinois, Minnesota, Nebraska, and Utah.

On October 5, 1851, approximately one year after Vice President Millard Fillmore succeeded to the presidency upon the death of Zachary Taylor, the Utah Territorial Legislature established Millard County, with Fillmore City as its county seat.

FRANKLIN PIERCE, FOURTEENTH PRESIDENT
1853-1857

There are towns named Pierce in Georgia, Nebraska, North Dakota, Washington, and Wisconsin. There is also a Pierceton, in Indiana.

Pierce County and City, Nebraska, were named in 1859 for Franklin Pierce, two years after he left the presidency.

An interesting comparison with modern costs is the 1870 tax list of Pierce County: The wealthiest resident had an assessed valuation of $779, and her taxes were $19.67. The citizen with the smallest assessed valuation was $33, and his taxes were $2.72.

There was a poll tax of two dollars for every voting man, and a one-dollar tax for everyone who owned a dog.

JAMES BUCHANAN, FIFTEENTH PRESIDENT
1857-1861

There are towns named Buchanan in Georgia, Iowa, Michigan, Missouri, New York, and Virginia.

Buchanan, Michigan, was named in honor of Senator James Buchanan, for his efforts in the United States Senate to attain statehood for Michigan. Statehood was granted in 1837, twenty years before Mr. Buchanan was inaugurated as fifteenth president.

ABRAHAM LINCOLN, SIXTEENTH PRESIDENT
1861-1865

There are towns named Lincoln in Colorado, Idaho, Kansas, Kentucky, Minnesota, Montana, Nebraska, Nevada, New Mexico, Oklahoma, Oregon, South Dakota, Washington, Wisconsin, and Wyoming. There is a Lincoln Heights in Ohio, and there are towns named Lincoln Park in Colorado, Michigan, New Jersey, and New York, as well as two in Pennsylvania.

ANDREW JOHNSON, SEVENTEENTH PRESIDENT
1865–1869

There are towns named Johnson in Arkansas, Georgia, Missouri, and Tennessee.

ULYSSES S. GRANT, EIGHTEENTH PRESIDENT
1869–1877

There are towns named Grant in Indiana, Kansas, Kentucky, Minnesota, Nebraska, New Mexico, North Dakota, Oklahoma, Oregon, South Dakota, Washington, West Virginia, and Wisconsin. There are also Grants Pass, Oregon, Grantsville, West Virginia, and Grantville, Kansas, and there are towns called Ulysses in Kansas, Kentucky, and Nebraska.

Grants Pass, Oregon, was named for the Civil War general by a road crew working in an area north of this point. This action was triggered by the news of Grant's capture of Vicksburg, Mississippi, on July 4, 1863.

After the Kansas county was named Grant, the county seat was dubbed Ulysses.

The town site of Ulysses, Nebraska, was laid in June, 1868, the year before Grant assumed the presidency.

When the Chicago, Burlington and Quincy Railroad announced that it would build a rail line through this area in Nebraska, a town sprang up. In 1886 it was named Grant, in honor of the former President.

RUTHERFORD B. HAYES, NINETEENTH PRESIDENT
1877–1881

There are towns named Hayes in Louisiana, South Dakota, and Virginia.

JAMES A. GARFIELD, TWENTIETH PRESIDENT
1881

There are towns named Garfield in Colorado, Kansas, Montana, Nebraska, New Jersey, Ohio, Oklahoma, Utah, and Washington.

Garfield, Kansas, originally a supply camp for the Santa Fe Railroad, was selected in 1872 by a three-man advance committee from Geneva, Ohio, for the location of their new colony. One year later, the settlers changed the name of their community from Camp Criley to Garfield, in honor of James A. Garfield, who had represented their former district in the House of Representatives.

When Congressman Garfield learned of this honor, he told the townspeople that he would donate a bell for the first church they erected. On March 7, 1876, the Congregation Church was dedicated, proud owner of the new Garfield bell.

In honor of the assassinated President, a railroad station (and later the city), on the New Jersey Bergen County Railroad was named Garfield in 1881.

President Garfield served only two months of his four-year term. He was mortally wounded by assassin Charles J. Guiteau on July 2 and died, after lingering four months, on September 19, 1881.

CHESTER A. ARTHUR, TWENTY-FIRST PRESIDENT
1881–1885

There are towns named Arthur in Illinois, Indiana, Nebraska, Nevada, North Dakota, Tennessee, Texas, and Wisconsin.

In 1881 the postal authorities asked the people of Arthur, North Dakota—then called Rosedale—to change the name of their town, because it was the same as that of another North Dakota locale. The townspeople decided to honor Chester Alan Arthur, who had recently become President.

GROVER CLEVELAND, TWENTY-SECOND AND TWENTY-FOURTH PRESIDENT
1885–1889 and 1893–1897

There are towns named Cleveland in Arkansas, Mississippi, Missouri, New York, North Carolina, Oklahoma, Tennessee, and Texas.

BENJAMIN HARRISON, TWENTY-THIRD PRESIDENT
1889–1893

See William Henry Harrison, ninth President, his grandfather.

WILLIAM McKINLEY, TWENTY-FIFTH PRESIDENT
1896–1901

There is a McKinley in Maine and a McKinleyville in California.

Mount McKinley, in Alaska, is the highest point on the North American continent, 20,320 feet—a fact not known until 1896. The mountain was named for the incumbent President, and the area became a national park in 1917.

THEODORE ROOSEVELT, TWENTY-SIXTH PRESIDENT
1901-1909

There are towns named Roosevelt in Arizona, Minnesota, Montana, New Jersey, New Mexico, New York, Oklahoma, Utah, and Washington.

WILLIAM H. TAFT, TWENTY-SEVENTH PRESIDENT
1909-1913

There are towns named Taft in California, Florida, Louisiana, Oklahoma, Oregon, and Tennessee.

WOODROW WILSON, TWENTY-EIGHTH PRESIDENT
1913-1921

There are towns named Wilson in Kentucky, Tennessee, and Texas, and towns named Woodrow in Arkansas, Minnesota, and Utah.

WARREN HARDING, TWENTY-NINTH PRESIDENT
1921-1923

There are towns named Harding in Minnesota, New Mexico, South Dakota, and West Virginia.

In 1900, four Polish families had settled in a small Minnesota community, where they established a small school. Twenty-three years later, they decided to rename their town Harding, after President Warren Harding, who had just died in office.

CALVIN COOLIDGE, THIRTIETH PRESIDENT
1923-1929

There are towns named Coolidge in Arizona, Georgia, Kansas, New Mexico, and Texas, and there is a Coolidge Dam in Arizona.

HERBERT HOOVER, THIRTY-FIRST PRESIDENT
1929–1933

There is a Hoover Dam on the Arizona-Nevada border.

FRANKLIN D. ROOSEVELT, THIRTY-SECOND PRESIDENT
1933–1945

There is a Roosevelttown, New York, and there's Franklin D. Roosevelt Lake in Washington.

American Presidents who took office after Franklin Roosevelt—Harry S. Truman (1945–1953), Dwight D. Eisenhower (1953–1961), John F. Kennedy (1961–1963), Lyndon B. Johnson (1963–1969), Richard M. Nixon (1969–1974), Gerald Ford (1974–1977), and Jimmy Carter—have not, as yet, had places named after them, with the exception of John F. Kennedy. After his assassination, a number of places took his name, the most famous being Cape Kennedy, Florida, site of the spacecraft launches. However, that name reverted to Cape Canaveral in 1973, and only the Kennedy Space Center, located on the cape, bears his name.

Coincidence Names

Most of the places that carry Presidents' names have been named specifically for them. However, many towns and cities bear the names of men who share a surname with a President. Such towns cannot claim to be true presidential namesakes, of course. The following are some examples:

QUINCY, MASSACHUSETTS

This was the hometown of John Adams, father of John Quincy Adams. It was named in 1792 for Colonel John Quincy, a grandfather of Abigail Smith Adams, John's wife. Their oldest son was named John Quincy after his great-grandfather.

HARRISON, ARKANSAS

This town was founded by Captain H. W. Fick and named for M. LaRue Harrison, who surveyed and plotted it in 1869.

FILLMORE, CALIFORNIA

This town was named after J. P. Fillmore, the general superintendent of the Southern Pacific Railroad Company. The region began to flourish after a railway was built there in 1886.

HAYESVILLE, NORTH CAROLINA

The town was named in 1861 for George Hayes, who was the state representative from Cherokee County to the North Carolina Assembly.

ARTHUR, KENTUCKY

In 1876 the post-office name was changed from Butcher Springs to Arthur for an early settler, Alexander A. Arthur.

CLEVELAND, TENNESSEE

The state legislature named this county seat after Colonel Benjamin Cleveland, a Revolutionary War hero.

Cleveland, Ohio, was named for Moses Cleaveland, who first surveyed the Western Reserve for the Connecticut Land Company, which settled the area in 1796.

TAFT, TEXAS

The town's name was changed from Mesquital to Taft for Mr. and Mrs. Charles Phelps Taft. They were stockholders in the Coleman-Fulton Pasture Company, the corporation that owned the site.

WILSON, NORTH CAROLINA

The town was named in honor of Brigadier General Louis Wilson, who died of a fever in Vera Cruz, Mexico, in 1847. He had organized a company of troops to join the United States Army in the Mexican War.

HOOVERSVILLE, PENNSYLVANIA

Jonas Hoover, after whom the town was named, was a son of George and Catherine Huber. He came to this region of Pennsylvania in the early 1830's.

TRUMANSBURG, NEW YORK

This was a land grant given to the soldier, Abner Tremain. He had changed his name to Treeman, but when he was granted a post office, a clerk mistakenly thought the hand-written pair of *e*'s in his name were a *u*, spelling Truman.

NIXON, TEXAS

The town was built near the newly constructed San Antonio and Gulf Railway on land owned by John T. Nixon.

 **4**

NAMES OF FAMOUS AMERICAN FIGURES

It took many people, from all walks of life, to build America. Navigators, explorers, frontiersmen, and pioneers prepared the land for settlers, farmers, craftsmen. Statesmen, politicians, jurists, and lawmen helped organize a large and diverse population into a nation living together in harmony. Men of medicine, fighters for human betterment, educators, and clergymen helped make our environment more meaningful. Inventors and scientists strove to improve our way of life. Journalists and writers gave us needed information and food for thought. And athletes and entertainers took our minds from our daily labors, enabling us to enjoy leisure.

In this chapter we are considering place names that honor famous Americans who helped shape the United States as it is today.

Explorers

COLUMBUS

There are towns named Columbus in Arkansas, Florida, Georgia, New York, Oregon, Washington, and Wisconsin. There's a Columbia in Alabama, Illinois, Maine, Missouri, and New Jersey; and a Columbiana in Alabama.

More than sixty places in the United States have been named in honor of the Admiral of the Ocean Sea. There are even several places that bear the name Isabella—in Georgia, Michigan, Oklahoma, Pennsylvania, and Tennessee.

LEWIS AND CLARK

There are towns named Lewis in Iowa, Missouri, New York, Washington, West Virginia, and Wisconsin, and towns named Lewisburg in Alabama and Tennessee. There is a Lewisport in Kentucky, a Lewiston in Illinois, and a Lewisville in both Arkansas and Idaho.

There are towns named Clark in Arkansas, Idaho, Illinois, Indiana, Kansas, Kentucky, Missouri, Nevada, Ohio, South Dakota, Washington, and Wisconsin, and towns named Clarksburg in Maryland and West Virginia. There's a Clarkston in Montana; and a Clarkesville in Arkansas, Florida, Missouri, and Tennessee.

Captain Meriwether Lewis and Lieutenant William Clark are best known for their expedition across the Louisiana Territory in 1804–1806. After the United States bought the territory from France, President Jefferson appointed the famous pair to explore the new land and pioneer an overland route to the Pacific. They reached the mouth of the Columbia River in November 1805, and returned to St. Louis the following year with much valuable data about the flora, fauna, and geography of the great West.

Frontiersmen

BOONE

There are towns named Boone in Arkansas, Illinois, Indiana, Iowa, Kentucky, Missouri, Nebraska, and West Virginia; and there are a Boonville and a Boonsboro in Missouri.

Daniel Boone, who lived from 1734 to 1820, helped lead settlers into new areas, crossing the Appalachian Mountains through the Cumberland Gap. He explored and settled Kentucky, then, when that state became too heavily populated, he moved west to Missouri, where he died in 1820, the year of that state's admission to the Union.

CARSON

There are towns named Carson in Alabama, California, Mississippi, and North Dakota. Theres a Carson City in Michigan and in Nevada, a Carsonville in Georgia, and a Kit Carson in Colorado.

Christopher "Kit" Carson was a guide, hunter, and soldier. In the

1840's he led John Frémont's exploratory party into the western territory, and later, during the Civil War, he helped the Union fight Indians in the Southwest.

Carson operated a trading post on the site that is now Kit Carson, Colorado. The locale, a main supply point for the great Southwest, led many stage companies and trading outfits to set up regional quarters there. The town was already flourishing when it became the terminus of the Kansas Pacific Railroad in 1870.

Here are some events that took place in Kit Carson and show the flavor of the times:

May 17, 1870. A railroad water tank was torn down by Indians, causing the army to send in three companies of U.S. cavalry.

December 7, 1871. The town was surrounded by thousands of buffalo.

January 20, 1872. Grand Duke Alexis of Russia hunted and killed five buffalo. In a state of excitement over his conquest, he hugged and kissed Colonel George Custer, his escort.

EARP

Wyatt Earp, the controversial lawman and opportunist, had, for many years, a cabin and a mine in California.

Earp's many occupations included stagecoach driver, railroad worker, buffalo hunter, assistant city marshal, gambling-casino owner, and prize fight referee.

He lived to the ripe old age of ninety in his Los Angeles home, dying in 1929.

Patriots

ADAMS

The town of Adams, Massachusetts, was incorporated in 1778 and named in honor of the hero of the independence movement, Samuel Adams.

Adams was the colonies' great propagandist. He was famous for, among other things, helping form the Sons of Liberty, masterminding the Boston Tea Party—a protest against England's granting the East India Company a tea monopoly in the colonies—and turning the Boston Massacre into a propaganda triumph for the Patriots.

REVERE

There are towns named Revere in Massachusetts, Minnesota, Missouri, and West Virginia.

Paul Revere did far more than just ride from Boston to Lexington on April 18, 1775, to warn John Hancock and Sam Adams that the British soldiers were coming to arrest them—as immortalized in Longfellow's long poem "The Midnight Ride of Paul Revere."

Revere's many exploits include serving as messenger for the Committee of Correspondence on many occasions and participating in the Boston Tea Party. He was an excellent silversmith (his work is still admired), and when the emergency caused a shortage of silver, he turned to copper engraving. He designed and printed the first issue of Continental money and designed and engraved the first official seal of the newly independent nation.

But that was only the beginning. Allowed to stroll through a government powder mill, he learned enough in a short visit to set up a mill for Massachusetts. When war came, he taught himself how to cast cannon. When the war was over, he formed the company known today as Revere Copper and took up plating. In 1795 he copper-bottomed the newly built U.S.S. *Constitution* and cast her ship's bell. He died in 1818, just as the age of steam was dawning.

HALE

There are towns named Hale in Colorado, Iowa, Kansas, Michigan, and Missouri.

Twenty-one-year-old Nathan Hale, an officer in the Continental Army, had volunteered for spy duty behind the British lines. He was captured and hanged in 1776.

Indian Leader

GERONIMO

There are towns named Geronimo in Arizona and Oklahoma.

Geronimo, one of the many great Indian leaders, was the wily war chieftain of the Chiricahua Apaches. Caught and forced to live on a reservation, Geronimo repeatedly escaped and formed new resistance bands. He finally surrendered to General Nelson Miles at Camp Bowie, Arizona, on September 4, 1886.

Men in Political Life

FRANKLIN

There are towns named Franklin in Alabama, Arkansas, Florida, Georgia, Idaho, Illinois, Indiana, Iowa, Kansas, Kentucky, Louisiana, Maine, Massachusetts, Michigan, Mississippi, Missouri, Nebraska, New Jersey, New York, North Carolina, Ohio, Oklahoma, Pennsylvania, Tennessee, Texas, Vermont, Virginia, and Washington. There is also a Franklinton in Florida; a Franklinville in New Jersey, New York, and North Carolina; a Frankton in Indiana; a Franktown in California; and a Frankville in Washington and Alabama.

The second-largest number of American places named for a single person, after George Washington, honor the Sage of Philadelphia, Benjamin Franklin.

The accomplishments of Franklin are legendary: invention of the lightning rod, the Franklin stove, and bifocal glasses; organization of the first circulating library and the first city fire and street-cleaning departments. Franklin was a signer of the Declaration of Independence, of the Treaty of Alliance with France, of the Treaty of Peace with England, and the United States Constitution.

A town in Pennsylvania was christened Franklin by state legislative enactment on April 18, 1795, five years after his death. Located at the crucial junction of the Allegheny River with French Creek and Oil Creek, Franklin, Pennsylvania, has probably been the site of more forts than any other locale in American history: Fort Machault (French, 1753); Fort Venango (English, 1760); Fort Franklin (United States, 1787); and Fort Old Garrison (United States, 1796).

HANCOCK

There are towns named Hancock in Georgia, Illinois, Indiana, Iowa, Kentucky, Maine, Maryland, Massachusetts, Michigan, Mississippi, Ohio, Tennessee, and West Virginia.

John Hancock was an early supporter of the Revolution, president of the Second Continental Congress, first signer of the Declaration of Independence, and the first governor of Massachusetts.

HAMILTON

There are towns named Hamilton in Florida, Illinois, Indiana, Iowa, Kansas, Kentucky, Mississippi, Nebraska, New York, Ohio, Oregon, Rhode Island, Tennessee, and Texas, and there's a Hamilton Park in Kentucky.

Alexander Hamilton, the first Secretary of the Treasury and a brilliant leader of the Federalists, was ultraconservative in his handling of the financial affairs of the new United States. His efforts, unpopular at the time, put the new nation on a solid economic footing and paid off all Revolutionary War debts to the penny.

In September 1791, Fort Hamilton, Ohio, was built and named for him. He died in a duel with Aaron Burr, at Weehawken, New Jersey, on July 11, 1804.

WEBSTER

There are towns named Webster in Georgia, Iowa, Kentucky, Louisiana, Massachusetts, Mississippi, Missouri, Nebraska, and West Virginia, and there's a Webster City in Iowa and a Websterville in Vermont.

Daniel Webster of Massachusetts had a long and distinguished career as a member of the House of Representatives, the Senate, and as Secretary of State. He was an articulate spokesman for a strong federal government, often opposing John C. Calhoun, an advocate of states' rights. His most famous quotation was made in the cause of a strong union: "Liberty and Union, now and forever, one and inseparable."

Samuel Slater, builder and operator of the first cotton-spinning machine in America, founded Webster, Massachusetts, in 1812, when he expanded his Pawtucket, Rhode Island, industry. A waterfall in the area gave him the necessary power for his new mill.

In later years, grateful townspeople, many of whom worked for Slater, wanted to name their home for him. He refused, suggesting instead a man he greatly admired—Daniel Webster, the great orator. His wishes were followed, and the act of incorporation for the town of Webster was passed on March 6, 1832.

CLAY

There are towns named Clay in Alabama, Arkansas, Florida, Georgia, Illinois, Indiana, Iowa, Kansas, Kentucky, Louisiana, Minnesota, Mississippi, Missouri, Nebraska, North Carolina, South Dakota, Tennessee, Texas, and West Virginia. There are towns named Clayton in Idaho, Illinois, New York, Ohio, and Wisconsin.

Henry Clay, as a member of the House and the Senate, won the title "The Great Compromiser" for his efforts to quell dissension between the North and the South. His legislative mediation helped bring about the Missouri Compromise of 1820 and the Compromise of 1850.

JEFFERSON DAVIS

There are towns named Jefferson Davis in Louisiana and Mississippi, and there's a Jeff Davis in Georgia and in Texas.

Jefferson Davis, president of the Confederacy, was born in Kentucky in 1808. Abraham Lincoln, his counterpart, was born one year later and one hundred miles away.

Prior to the war, Davis had served in the House, the Senate, and as Secretary of War.

CALHOUN

There are towns named Calhoun in Alabama, Arkansas, Florida, Georgia, Illinois, Iowa, Michigan, Mississippi, South Carolina, Texas, and West Virginia.

The people of the Georgia town built on the site of the Cherokee Indian village Othcaloga decided to call itself Calhoun in June 1850. This was in honor of John C. Calhoun, South Carolina Senator, Secretary of War, Vice President under John Quincy Adams and Andrew Jackson, Secretary of State, and the recognized spokesman for the states'-rights position. He had died earlier that year.

DOUGLAS

There are towns named Douglas in Alabama, Colorado, Georgia, Illinois, Kansas, Minnesota, Missouri, Nebraska, Nevada, Oklahoma, Oregon, South Dakota, Washington, and Wisconsin.

Stephen A. Douglas, the Little Giant of American politics, is best known for his popular-sovereignty position on the extension of slavery. He proposed, in a series of debates with Abraham Lincoln, that the residents of a particular territory be allowed to decide for themselves if they wanted slavery in their region. He was running against Lincoln for the United States

Senate. His states'-rights position on slavery made him a hero in the South, leading many southern towns to name themselves after him.

Douglas, Georgia, was established and became the county seat in 1858, the year of the famous Lincoln-Douglas debates. It's located in Coffee County, named for another historic figure, General John Coffee, of the War of 1812 fame.

BENTON

There are towns named Benton in Arkansas, Illinois, Indiana, Iowa, Kentucky, Minnesota, Mississippi, Missouri, Oregon, Pennsylvania, Tennessee, and Washington. There's a Benton Ridge in Ohio, and a Bentonville in Ohio and in Virginia.

Thomas Hart Benton, soldier, founder of the *Missouri Inquirer*, and United States Senator for thirty years, lived in Tennessee for a brief period. While the Democratic party was in control of the Tennessee legislature, it stipulated that the town of Benton be created in Polk County. This was probably a result of Benton's friendship with Tennessean Andrew Jackson (whom he had once shot in a street brawl).

Benton's daughter Jessie married John C. Frémont, the Pathfinder, and his grandnephew and namesake was one of America's great painters, especially of simple people and rural life.

CASS

There are towns named Cass in Illinois, Indiana, Iowa, Michigan, Minnesota, Missouri, Nebraska, North Dakota, and Texas.

Lewis Cass had a long and varied career in the service of the United States. He was an officer in the War of 1812, Secretary of War under Jackson, Governor of Michigan Territory, United States Senator, and Democratic presidential candidate in 1848.

Jurist

MARSHALL

There are towns named Marshall in Alabama, Illinois, Indiana, Iowa, Kansas, Kentucky, Michigan, Minnesota, Mississippi, North Carolina, Oklahoma, South Dakota, Tennessee, Texas, and West Virginia. There's a Marshallville in Ohio, and a Marshfield in Maine, Massachusetts, Vermont, and Wisconsin.

John Marshall, who fought throughout the hardest part of the Revolutionary War as an officer in a line regiment, was Secretary of State to John Adams, and a member of the House of Representatives, before accepting appointment from Adams (one of his last presidential acts) as fourth Chief Justice of the United States Supreme Court.

Marshall held that position from 1801 to 1835, and he virtually created the court as we know it, forcing acceptance of his philosophy, which called for a strong central government, and the right of the Supreme Court to pass on the constitutionality of Congressional enactments.

Humanitarians

BARTON

Barton, Kansas, was named after Clara Barton, affectionately called the Angel of the Battlefield by Union soldiers, whom she and three thousand other women volunteers nursed during the Civil War. They worked under the leadership of Dorothea Dix, who had been appointed Superintendent of Nurses.

Later, inspired by the work of the Swiss philanthropist Jean Henri Dunant, who founded the International Red Cross in 1864, Miss Barton strongly advocated and finally succeeded in founding an American affiliate in 1881 and established its traditions of disaster relief.

GARRISON

There are towns named Garrison in Iowa, Kentucky, and New York.

William Lloyd Garrison, the famous abolitionist leader, advocated many causes, including Indian rights and women's suffrage. His stance against slavery was voiced in *The Liberator*, and it was implemented in the American Anti-Slavery Society—both founded by him in the early 1830's.

Educator

BOOKER T. WASHINGTON

Mount Booker, Washington, was named for Booker T. Washington, who rose from slavery to become a leading educator of his time, founding the Tuskegee Institute in Alabama, an industrial school for black people.

Social Scientist

SCHOOLCRAFT

Schoolcraft, Michigan, was named for Henry Rowe Schoolcraft, famed ethnologist and one of the first Americans to make a serious study of Indian life and customs. In 1827, Schoolcraft purchased a great deal of rich prairie land here for $1.25 an acre.

Clergyman

HARVARD

John Harvard, an English clergyman who came to America in 1637, left his library and half his estate to the college recently founded in the Puritan colony of Massachusetts Bay. In 1639 the legislature voted to name the school, primarily devoted to training men for the ministry, Harvard College. There are towns named Harvard in Illinois, Massachusetts, and Nebraska.

Capitalist

ASTOR

There are towns named Astoria in Illinois, Oregon, South Dakota, and Wyoming.

John Jacob Astor, German-born American, founded the American Fur Company in the early part of the nineteenth century. The company developed a thriving business in peltry throughout the Pacific Northwest, and Astor became immensely rich. Other Astor speculations involved buying vast amounts of Manhattan land.

Inventors

FULTON

There are towns named Fulton in Arkansas, Georgia, Illinois, Indiana, Kentucky, Missouri, New York, Ohio, and Pennsylvania.

Robert Fulton began a new phase of transportation when he perfected the steamboat. His *Clermont*, a 133-foot long, eighteen-foot wide, paddlewheel steamboat, sailed up New York's Hudson River in the summer of 1807, taking thirty hours to travel 150 miles. It was named for the country estate of Robert R. Livingston, situated on the Hudson not far from the modern town of Clermont. Livingston had supported Fulton throughout the expensive process of developing the new vessel.

EDISON

There are towns named Edison in Georgia, New Jersey, Ohio, and Washington.

Thomas A. Edison, the Wizard of Menlo Park, was an ingenious individual who, with the help of many assistants, perfected hundreds of inventions. Some of these include telegraphy, mimeograph, police and fire instant callboxes, phonograph, carbon transmitter, incandescent lamp, motion-picture camera, projector, talking motion picture, alkaline storage battery, telescribe, and transophone. His total number of patents exceeded 1,100.

Scientist

EINSTEIN

Mount Einstein, Alaska, is named for Albert Einstein, Nobel prize winner in physics and architect of the theory of relativity. It seems appropriate that a mountain was named after Einstein.

Journalist

GREELEY

There are towns named Greeley in Colorado, Iowa, Kansas, Missouri, and Nebraska.

Horace Greeley was founder of the New York *Tribune*, an opponent of slavery, and an unsuccessful Democratic Presidential opponent of U.S. Grant in 1872.

An entire region in Kansas was named in honor of the newspaperman who put out the famed *Tribune*. Tribune, Kansas, is located in Greeley County. Nearby is another small town named Horace. A railroad siding was named Whitelaw, and a regional town was called Reid, both of them for the newspaper's editor, Whitelaw Reid.

Athlete

JIM THORPE

Jim Thorpe, Pennsylvania, was named after Jim Thorpe, the great football, baseball, and track star. Thorpe was born on a Sac and Fox Indian reservation in Oklahoma in 1888. His triumph in the 1912 Olympics was marred when Olympic officials discovered that he had once played a summer of semipro baseball and rescinded his honors.

In 1954, the town of Mauch Chunk changed its name to honor him. Thorpe is entombed there in a twenty-ton granite mausoleum, which is engraved with the words that King Gustav of Sweden said to him after he won both the pentathlon and the decathlon: "Sir, you are the greatest athlete in the world."

Thorpe was awed by no one, however august. His response to this royal tribute was a cheerful "Thanks, King."

Writers

THOREAU

Thoreau, New Mexico, was named after essayist and poet Henry David Thoreau. Thoreau believed in living simply and close to nature, which he did for a while near Walden Pond, Massachusetts. *Walden* is a journal of his experiences. His Essay "Resistance to Civil Government" influenced many, including India's great nationalist and spiritual leader, Mahatma Gandhi.

EMERSON

Mount Emerson, California, is named after Ralph Waldo Emerson, who left the ministry in 1832 to lecture and write essays, poetry, short articles, and books about his philosophical beliefs. He often spoke and wrote about transcendentalism, a Kantian philosophy in which, it is believed, certain knowledge is beyond the limits of experience.

TWAIN-HARTE

The town of Twain-Harte in California was named for the writers Mark Twain (Samuel Langhorne Clemens) and Bret Harte.

Clemens' most famous works are *The Adventures of Tom Sawyer*, and *The Adventures of Huckleberry Finn*. As a youngster he heard riverboat men calling out "mark twain," meaning that the water was two fathoms deep. Liking the sound of the words, Clemens adopted it for his pen name.

Bret Harte, born in New York City in 1836, wrote stories about the West, the most famous being "The Luck of Roaring Camp."

NAMES OF MILITARY PERSONALITIES

The nation as a whole, and all sections within it, have placed America's military personalities in a special category. This is reflected by the many towns and cities that are named in honor of these men—officers who have fought in American wars, ranging from the eighteenth to the twentieth centuries. It's the people's way of paying tribute to those who, they believe, have defended them and their freedoms.

French and Indian War (1754–1763)

SCHUYLER

There are towns named Schuyler in Illinois, Missouri, and New York.

After General Philip Schuyler served in the French and Indian War and the Revolution, he became involved in the political arena. He was a delegate and then a member of the Continental Congress, and one of the first two senators that New York sent to the new Congress following ratification of the Constitution in 1789. He was also Alexander Hamilton's father-in-law.

American Revolution (1775-1783)

ETHAN ALLEN

The people of Hero Islands, a northwestern part of Vermont, paid tribute to two native sons, Ethan and Ira Allen, heroes of the Revolutionary War, by naming these islands North Hero and South Hero.

Ethan's most famous exploit occurred on May 10, 1775, when he led his group of fighting men, the Green Mountain Boys, in a surprise attack on the skeleton garrison at Fort Ticonderoga. (In co-command was Colonel Benedict Arnold of Connecticut.) When the bewildered King's officer demanded to know in whose name he was being asked to surrender the fort, Allen thundered his famous reply: "In the name of the Great Jehovah and the Continental Congress."

Later, during a battle in Montreal, Allen was captured and held for a while as a prisoner of war in England.

MERCER

There are towns named Mercer in Illinois, Kentucky, Missouri, New Jersey, North Dakota, Ohio, Pennsylvania, and West Virginia. There's a Mercersburg in Pennsylvania.

General Hugh Mercer, a Scottish-born physician, was killed in the Battle of Princeton on January 3, 1777.

MONTGOMERY

There are towns named Montgomery in Alabama, Arkansas, Georgia, Illinois, Indiana, Iowa, Kansas, Kentucky, Maryland, Mississippi, Missouri, New York, North Carolina, Ohio, Pennsylvania, Tennessee, Texas, and Virginia.

General Richard Montgomery, born in Ireland, had earlier served with the British Army. After he came to America he was given a command in the Revolutionary forces, and soon demonstrated his ability by capturing Montreal. He was killed while leading an assault on Quebec on December 31, 1775.

MORGAN

There are towns named Morgan in Alabama, Arkansas, Colorado, Georgia, Illinois, Indiana, Kansas, Kentucky, Missouri, Ohio, Tennessee, Vermont, and West Virginia.

General Daniel Morgan, born in New Jersey, fought in many Revolutionary War battles. In 1794 he commanded the Virginia militia, which helped suppress the Whiskey Rebellion in western Pennsylvania.

WARREN

There are towns named Warren in Georgia, Illinois, Indiana, Iowa, Kentucky, Mississippi, Missouri, New Jersey, New York, North Carolina, Ohio, Pennsylvania, Tennessee, and Virginia. There's also a Warrens in Wisconsin, and a Warrensburg in Missouri.

General Joseph Warren, a physician in private life, was an important early Patriot. On June 17, 1775, although he held a commission as major general of Massachusetts troops, Warren served as a private soldier in the fighting on Bunker (or Breed's) Hill. He was killed in the final assault.

Two months earlier, Warren had been responsible for sending Paul Revere and William Dawes to Lexington to warn Hancock and Adams of their imminent danger.

Foreign Officers in the Revolution

LAFAYETTE

There are towns named Lafayette in Arkansas, Florida, Louisiana, Mississippi, Missouri, and Wisconsin; and towns named Fayette in Alabama, Georgia, Illinois, Indiana, Iowa, Kentucky, Mississippi, Ohio, Pennsylvania, Tennessee, Texas, and West Virginia. There are towns named Fayetteville in Arkansas, Pennsylvania, North Carolina, and Tennessee.

Marie Joseph Paul Ives Roch Gilbert du Motier, the young Marquis de Lafayette, ranks with two native-born Americans, George Washington and Benjamin Franklin, in having the greatest number of towns named for him.

Commissioned a major general in the Continental Army, Lafayette was not only a close adviser to General Washington but went back to France in 1778 to win support for the American cause.

In 1778, Cross Creek, North Carolina, and her neighboring settlement, Campbelltown, united under the name of Upper and Lower Cross Creek. Five years later, the North Carolina General Assembly decided to rename the city Fayetteville, in honor of the young French nobleman.

When Lafayette visited this city in 1825, he was given a grand welcome and a townwide celebration. The coach he rode in has been preserved and is now on public display.

STEUBEN

There are towns named Steuben in Indiana, Maine, Michigan, New York, and Wisconsin, and there's a Steubenville in Indiana and Ohio.

Baron Friedrich von Steuben, a Prussian officer and formerly aide-de-camp to Frederick the Great, was recommended to General Washington by Benjamin Franklin. In early 1778, Washington made him inspector general of the Continental Army, responsible for its training and reorganizing.

Rewriting and simplifying the complicated manual of arms, Steuben threw himself into the training program with infectious zeal. Within a few weeks he had introduced order and discipline into the chaotic training program and simultaneously won the hearts of his men. He is regarded as possibly history's only popular drillmaster.

Steuben remained in the United States after the war, becoming a naturalized citizen in 1783.

PULASKI

There are towns named Pulaski in Arkansas, Georgia, Illinois, Iowa, Indiana, Kentucky, Missouri, and Virginia.

General Casimir Pulaski, a Polish military officer, was put in command of a Revolutionary cavalry corps. He was killed in battle in Savannah, Georgia, in 1779.

KOSCIUSKO

There are towns named Kosciusko in Mississippi and Indiana.

The Polish engineering officer Thaddeus Kosciusko served with the Revolutionary forces from 1776 to 1783. He laid out the American defenses at Saratoga and Yorktown and designed the first fortifications at West Point. He then returned to Poland, becoming commander in chief of the Polish army in 1794.

War of 1812 (1812–1815)

PERRY

There are towns named Perry in Alabama, Arkansas, Florida, Georgia, Illinois, Indiana, Kansas, Kentucky, Maine, Mississippi, Missouri, Ohio, Pennsylvania, Tennessee, plus Perrydale in Oregon and Perryopolis in Pennsylvania.

The towns and counties were named for Captain Oliver Hazard Perry, victor at the Battle of Lake Erie, September 10, 1813. During the battle his flagship, the *Lawrence*, was so battered that he had to be rowed to the *Niagara*, where he continued the fight. His victory left the way clear for an American invasion of Canada, and to report the fact to army commander William Henry Harrison, Perry dispatched his famous laconic message: "We have met the enemy, and they are ours."

PIKE

There are towns named Pike in Alabama, Arkansas, Georgia, Illinois, Indiana, Kentucky, Mississippi, Missouri, Ohio, Pennsylvania, plus Pikes Peak in Colorado, Pikesville in Maryland and Kentucky, and Pikeville in North Carolina.

General Zebulon Pike, explorer and army officer, was killed in the assault on York (now Toronto), Ontario, on April 27, 1813.

RIPLEY

There are towns named Ripley in California, Illinois, Maine, Mississippi, Missouri, Ohio, Oklahoma, Tennessee, and West Virginia.

Eleazar W. Ripley served as a general in the War of 1812, sometimes called the Second War of Independence. Two decades later he ran for and won a seat in the House of Representatives.

Ripley, Ohio, on the Ohio River, was the site of a famous way station on the Underground Railroad. Perhaps its best known "client" was the fictional Eliza Harris in *Uncle Tom's Cabin*, who crossed to it from Kentucky on the ice floes.

TECUMSEH

There are towns named Tecumseh in Kansas, Michigan, Nebraska, and Oklahoma, plus the Tecumseh Mountains in New Hampshire.

The Shawnee word *tecumseh* means "the flight of a comet across the sky" or "the spring of a panther from a tree limb"—both denoting a sweeping arc through space. This was a fitting description for the Shawnee chieftain Tecumseh who, in an attempt to win back what his people had lost to the whites, joined forces with the British in the War of 1812. He was killed at the Battle of the Thames (Ontario, Canada), on October 5, 1813.

Another namesake of the great chief was General W. T. Sherman, who was originally named Tecumseh and called Cump. "William" was added later by a shocked foster mother, who insisted that the boy have a Christian first name.

Texas War of Independence (1836)

HOUSTON

There are towns named Houston in Alabama, Arkansas, Georgia, Minnesota, Mississippi, Missouri, Pennsylvania, Tennessee, and Texas.

Sam Houston became a permanent hero of the new Republic of Texas when his troops decisively beat General Santa Anna's army at the Battle of San Jacinto on April 21, 1836.

Houston was deeply involved in politics before and after he became a Texan. The offices he held included member of the House of Representatives, governor of Tennessee, first president of Texas, senator from Texas, and governor of the state of Texas from 1859 to 1861.

The Congress of the Republic of Texas approved a petition on June 12, 1837, which named the first Texas county for him. The county seat was called Crockett, after the Tennessee scout David Crockett, who had camped near the area while en route to the Alamo, where he was killed in 1836.

The city of Houston, in Harris County, was named for Sam by the Allen brothers, settlers in the region. This was the first capital of the new Republic until Austin was given that distinction four years later, in 1840.

Mexican War (1846-1848)

SCOTT

There are towns named Scott in Arkansas, Illinois, Indiana, Iowa, Kansas, Kentucky, Louisiana, Minnesota, Mississippi, Missouri, Tennessee, Virginia, plus Scottsboro, Alabama, Scottsburg, Oregon, Scottsville in New York and Michigan, and Fort Scott, Kansas.

General Winfield Scott, a veteran of many battles, won an impressive victory in the Mexican War when his troops captured Vera Cruz, in March 1847, and then went to rack up a string of victories that resulted in the capitulation of the capital, Mexico City, on September 14.

He tried his hand at politics when he ran, as the Whig candidate, for President in 1852. He lost to Franklin Pierce by 215,000 popular votes and 212 electoral votes.

Civil War (1861-1865)

FRÉMONT

There are towns named Fremont in Colorado, Idaho, Indiana, Nebraska, Vermont, and Wyoming.

John C. Frémont, the Pathfinder of the West, was more successful as an explorer and politician than as a military general. In 1842 he won fame for mapping the Oregon Trail. Eight years later he was elected to the United States Senate, one of the first two senators that California sent to that body. His career rapidly progressed when the newly formed Republican party chose him as its presidential nominee in 1856. He ran unsuccessfully as a free-soil candidate against James Buchanan, opposing the expansion of slavery into the territories.

In 1862, as a major general in the Civil War, he issued an emancipation proclamation, freeing the slaves in the region under his military command. This was overstepping his authority, and the order was rescinded by President Lincoln, who soon after issued one of his own on January 1, 1863.

HANCOCK

Hancock, Minnesota, was named after Winfield Scott Hancock, who made his mark as a corps commander in the Union victory at Gettysburg, defending the position against which George Pickett made his famous charge. As the Democratic presidential candidate in 1880, he ran a strong campaign against James A. Garfield, losing by fewer than ten thousand votes out of a total of nine million cast.

JACKSON

There are towns named Stonewall in Arkansas, Georgia, Louisiana, Mississippi, North Carolina, and Oklahoma.

General Thomas Jonathan Jackson won the sobriquet "Stonewall" at the Battle of Bull Run, Virginia, on July 21, 1861, where his Virginia troops withstood an unnerving Union flank attack. Confederate Bernard E. Bee, trying to rally his own shaken men, pointed out Jackson's steadiness: "There is Jackson standing like a stone wall."

Two years later, after the Confederate victory at the bloody battle of Chancellorsville, Jackson was accidentally killed by his own troops.

LEE

There are towns named Lee in Alabama, Arkansas, Florida, Georgia, Illinois, Iowa, Kentucky, Mississippi, North Carolina, South Carolina, Texas, and Virginia.

Robert E. Lee, the brilliant commander in chief of the Confederate Army, was originally offered command of the Union forces. But he chose to go with Virginia, his beloved home state.

After the Civil War he assumed the presidency of Washington College, Virginia—now Washington and Lee University—holding the position until his death in 1870. Lee is generally conceded to have been America's finest soldier.

SHERMAN

There are towns named Sherman in Kansas, Nebraska, and Oregon.

General William T. Sherman evoked the bitter hatred of the South with his famous March to the Sea. After the fall of Atlanta in the summer of

1864, Sherman had to decide whether to advance with his victorious army into the heart of the South or to retreat. He chose to advance. On November 15, 1864, he led his troops out of Atlanta on a march to Savannah and the sea that devastated an area three hundred miles long and sixty miles wide.

Later, in 1869, he succeeded U.S. Grant, who had been elected President, as general and commander in chief of the Army.

SHERIDAN

There are towns named Sheridan in Arkansas, Indiana, Kansas, Michigan, Montana, Nebraska, North Dakota, and Wyoming.

General Philip Sheridan, Union cavalry commander, was epitomized in Thomas Buchanan Read's poem "Sheridan's Ride," for his punishing twenty-mile gallop from Winchester to Cedar Creek, Virginia, to rally retreating troops.

Indian Wars

WAYNE

There are towns named Wayne in Georgia, Illinois, Indiana, Iowa, Kentucky, Michigan, Mississippi, Missouri, Nebraska, New York, North Carolina, Ohio, Pennsylvania, Tennessee, Utah, and West Virginia, plus Waynesboro, Pennsylvania, Waynesburg, Kentucky, Waynesville in Missouri and Ohio, and Waynetown, Indiana.

Anthony Wayne received the nickname "Mad Anthony" during the Revolutionary War, for the daring assault he led on the post at Stony Point, New York, in 1779.

Long after the war, on August 20, 1794, General Wayne defeated more than 1,500 Shawnee, Miami, Ottawa, Chippewa, Potawatomi, and Fox Indians in the famous Battle of Fallen Timbers near Maumee, Ohio.

The battle took its name from the site of a tornado's swath, which had tumbled forest trees every which way, where Wayne chose to attack the waiting Indians. His men outnumbered them two to one and were skilled in forest fighting. He gave them only one order: "Charge the damn rascals with the bayonet."

CUSTER

There are towns named Custer in Colorado, Indiana, Kentucky, Michigan, Montana, Nebraska, Oklahoma, and South Dakota.

George A. Custer is best remembered for his disastrous defeat on the shores of the Little Bighorn River, Wyoming, on June 25, 1876. He and two hundred men from the famous Seventh Cavalry were annihilated by a force of 2,500 to 4,000 warriors, probably the largest Indian army ever assembled in the United States.

Spanish-American War (1898)

DEWEY

There are towns named Dewey in Oklahoma and South Dakota, plus Deweyville, in Texas.

Commodore George Dewey struck the first blow in the Spanish-American War when his small fleet destroyed a squadron of archaic Spanish ships in Manila Bay, Philippines, on May 1, 1898. No Americans were killed—although one man died of heat stroke—but there were 381 Spanish casualties.

World War I (1917-1918)

PERSHING

There are towns named Pershing in Indiana, Missouri, and Nevada.

In 1916 General John J. Pershing first achieved prominence as the commander of a force that pursued the bandit Pancho Villa into Mexico with singular lack of success. During the following year, after American entrance into World War I, Pershing was appointed head of the American Expeditionary Force.

In 1932 he won a Pulitizer Prize for his memoirs, *My Experiences in the World War*.

NAMES OF INDIAN ORIGIN

Indians have given a great deal to humankind. Their rich culture, consisting of songs, stories, handicrafts, languages, family and tribal customs, and physical accomplishments, will never vanish from American history.

These amazing, hardy people came from Siberia across the Bering Strait (probably then a land bridge) to Alaska some 25,000 years ago. They then migrated to all parts of North and South America, eventually establishing hundreds of tribes in communities.

Indians lived off the land. They were the land, and the land was part of them. The brown earth, the blue sky, the sun, moon, clouds, and all the wildlife were interwoven into the bodies and minds of the Indian people. Thus, it is no surprise that the names these first Americans gave to many parts of the continent were a reflection of how they lived and what they thought.

Love Stories

TUCUMCARI, NEW MEXICO

According to Indian legend, an old Apache chief felt it was time his beautiful daughter Kari married. He chose two possible husbands from his tribe, one of whom would marry Kari and eventually take his place as chief. Kari was in love with one of the braves—Tocom, but hated the other—Tonapon.

It was decided that the young men would fight with daggers to the death, the winner marrying Kari. The time came, and the fight began, with

Kari secretly watching from a distance. When she saw Tocom slain, she rushed toward Tonapon, killing him and herself, her body falling across her loved one. As soon as the old chief heard what had happened, he too plunged a dagger into his heart, yelling in anguish: "Tocom-kari."

EAGLE LAKE, TEXAS

Two young Karankawa braves were in love with the same Indian maiden, but she could not choose which one she would marry. To settle the affair, it was decided that the first man to cross the lake and come back with an eagle would win the squaw's hand.

MAIDEN ROCK, WISCONSIN

This town, near a high, four-mile-wide rock formation that overlooks a lovely lake, got its name from an Indian legend.

According to the tale, the beautiful Indian maiden Winona was told by her chieftain father that she had to marry Kewanee, a young chief of the friendly Dakota tribe. She refused because she loved and was secretly meeting White Eagle, who was one of the enemy Chippewas. Her father, furious, sent his braves to kill White Eagle. Learning of this, Winona ran to the rock to warn her lover, but could not stop the arrow that pierced his heart. Seeing what had happened, she took him in her arms and leaped into the lake below, choosing to die with him. Thereafter, the place was known as Maiden Rock.

Religion

DIABLO, CALIFORNIA

In 1806 a Spanish military expedition from San Francisco marched against a tribe of Indians they identified as the Bolgones. The Indians were encamped at the foot of a large mountain, and when opposing forces met, the battle took place in front of a cavelike part of this mountain. Suddenly, in the midst of fighting, something quite strange occurred—a figure that looked like a spirit, decorated with the most extraordinary plumage and making all kinds of strange movements, appeared among the combatants. At this point, the Indians fought harder and easily won. The spirit then departed toward the mountain. The Spaniards, upon learning that the spirit went through the same ceremony daily, named the mountain "Diablo," which was their translation of *puy* (evil spirit), a name they heard the Indians call it.

SUNDANCE, WYOMING

Near the town that became known as Sundance is a large mountain that the Indians called *Wi Wacippi Paha*, meaning Temple of the Sioux. It is said that dances to the sun were offered on top of this granite giant, thus giving it and the town its present name.

The sun was very important in the lives of the Plains Indians, and they went to great extremes to thank it for past favors and ask it for supernatural powers over their enemies.

Harry Longabaugh, a member of Butch Cassidy's Wild Bunch, also took his name from this town. He was known as the Sundance Kid.

THUNDERBOLT, GEORGIA

Centuries ago, during a heavy summer rainstorm, a giant thunderbolt of lightning struck near an Indian village. Everyone ran to the spot where it hit, wanting to see what the spirits had done. They saw a mineral spring that smelled like sulfur and iron, leading them to believe that it had been created by the thunderbolt.

Later, in the 1700's, the Reverend John Wesley, clergyman of the Church of England and founder of Methodism, came to Georgia to serve as minister in Savannah and as missionary to the Indians. He often visited Thunderbolt, walking the four miles from Savannah to preach to the settlers and their servants and to teach them hymns.

SHOSHONE, IDAHO

Idaho was the home of the Shoshone and Bannock Indians, who roamed the area of the Snake River, fishing for salmon and digging camas roots. Sacagawea, the Bird Woman, who guided Lewis and Clark through the Rocky Mountains, her infant on her back, was a Shoshone.

Later, cowboys drove their cattle to the Snake River Plains for the winter, passing through Shoshone. The discovery of silver and lead in 1878 made Shoshone a fast-growing wild town. It had twelve saloons, dancing on every street corner, frequent gun fights, gambling places galore, and a busy jail, which was nothing more than a large hole in the ground with guards around it.

Water

MEDICINE LODGE, KANSAS

A long time ago, the Kiowa Indians traveled, once a year, to this part of Kansas to stay at a special river that they discovered had healing powers. Each year they would come, set up camp, bathe in the river, and drink its laxative mineral waters.

On the banks of the river they built a great "medicine lodge" in which they placed healing herbs on top of heated rocks. They would then pour the river's "magic" water over the herbs, creating steam, in which they sweated, as in a sauna.

Modern science has recognized the worth of many Indian cures. Today, more than two hundred herb and root medicines are used by medical doctors.

It was also at Medicine Lodge, Kansas, that the world-famous fighter against saloons, Carry A. Nation, started her campaign. At the turn of the century, this determined woman, armed with hatchet and Bible, set out all alone to rid the country of "the joints."

WALLA WALLA, WASHINGTON

The description of the land in which a tribe lived often became its name. Thus, the Walla Walla Indians got their name from the cascades that ran through their region. They called the rapidly flowing river *Walla Walla*, which meant "little swift river."

PAWTUCKET, RHODE ISLAND

The Narraganset Indians lived in Pawtucket long before the area was settled by white people. In Algonkian, the name means "falls of water."

The natural water power in the area enabled settlers to build mills, beginning with the sawmill built by Joseph Jensks, Jr., in 1671.

It was in Pawtucket that Samuel Slater gave the American cotton-manufacturing industry its start. He had worked in England for Richard Arkwright, inventor of the mechanical spinning frame, and wanted to introduce this new process in America. Since English law prohibited the export of models or drawings of such machinery, Slater simply memorized it.

In 1793, he came to Pawtucket and built a mill, using the first spinning frames ever employed on the North American continent. His wife, Hannah Wilkinson Slater, founded the cotton-thread industry here. She proved that thread spun from cotton fiber was stronger than the commonly used linen.

TY TY, GEORGIA

During the 1800's, in this southern part of Georgia, the Indians roamed up and down a small creek that was overgrown with thick evergreen bushes. The bushes had branches that intertwined, making it very difficult to get through. The local tribe came to call them tied-tight bushes, and the creek and town became known as Ti Ti or Ty Ty.

TUMWATER, WASHINGTON

Tumwater is the Chinook word for "falling water," an apt description of the cascades of the Deschutes River in the state of Washington. The Chinooks, an Indian people on the north bank of the Columbia River, lived in this region thousands of years before the first white settlers came.

WEEPING WATER, NEBRASKA

Indians in this part of the prairie, coming upon a sparkling, clear creek, named it *Nigahoe*, or "rustling water" because of the sound of water running over low falls. It was later mistranslated on an 1802 French map as *L'Eau qui pleure*—"the water that weeps." The log of of the Lewis and Clark expedition also referred to this creek, which flows into the Missouri, as Weeping Water.

OTTERTAIL, MINNESOTA

Before there were roads in frontier areas, a good way to travel was by water. This is how, in 1750, the first explorers in this region, a Frenchman and an Englishman, got around. During their explorations they met a band of Indians who showed them a body of water that the Frenchman translated as *lac de la queue de la loutre*—"the lake of the otter's tail." The Indians had named it this because there was a sandbar in the shape of an otter's tail at the point where the river flowed into the lake. It's still there today, more than two centuries later.

The town began to develop when Donald McDonald opened a trading post in 1849. He married an Indian princess by the name of Aunt Genevieve, who helped deliver many of the settlers' children.

Growing rapidly, the city in 1870 boasted of a population of twelve hundred, a weekly newspaper, five hotels, twenty-seven saloons, many stores, five lawyers, and a mail stage route.

COOS BAY, OREGON

The Kusan Indian word *coos* or *kusa* probably meant "lake" or "lagoon" or "inland bay." Lewis and Clark, exploring this region in 1805, estimated the Coos tribe to be about fifteen hundred in number.

The Indian tribes in this fertile area had a virtual paradise before white people—explorers, fur trappers, gold prospectors, and finally settlers—invaded their Garden of Eden. Game of all kinds abounded in the forest, the rivers were full of salmon and other fish, and vegetation of every kind grew profusely in the mild, humid coastal climate.

Wildlife and Hunting

BLACKDUCK, MINNESOTA

Every autumn thousands of black ducks would descend from the sky onto one of their favorite eating places, a beautiful Minnesota lake. The sky was so blackened by this natural occurrence that the Indians called the area Blackduck. The name was also taken by a prominent Chippewa chief who lived on the north side of Blackduck Lake with his tribe.

TWISP, WASHINGTON

Before this area was populated by white settlers, the Indians traveled over the Loop Loop Trail into a valley that was their hunting grounds. There they gathered game, berries, roots, mushrooms, and fish to stock their winter storage bins.

The valley was rich with vegetation and flowers of all sorts, which helped sustain large numbers of bees. The Indians called these little nature helpers *twisp*, which meant "yellow-jacket" or "buzzing of the bee."

The weather in this region, from the time of the Indians to the present, varies greatly from season to season. Temperatures can range from 50 degrees below zero in winter (with snow piling three to eight feet) to a summer heat exceeding 100 degrees.

CHUGWATER, WYOMING

In early days, the Plains Indians, in order to get their winter meat supply, would round up herds of buffalo and stampede them over high bluffs to their deaths. The sound of their bodies striking the earth below formed a "chug." The stream in the valley thus became known as "the land where the buffalo chug," or Chugwater.

The Indians would then proceed to butcher these dead bison, often making use of each part of their bodies. They used the flesh for food, the skin for shelter and clothing, the bones for tools and weapons, the horns for powder flasks, the hair for horse bridles and halters, and the dung for fuel.

The buffalo, once numbering sixty million, shrank to an unbelievable thirty-nine in 1900—a result of white man's massacre. Today, approximately thirty thousand live in protected areas.

Leaders

RED WING, MINNESOTA

The Mdewakanton, a tribe of the Santee Dakota, had their villages here at the head of Lake Pepin in the Mississippi River. Four great chiefs of this tribe were called *Koo-poo-hoo-sha*, meaning "wing of the wild swan dyed scarlet." The name of the town came from this colorful symbol.

COS COB, CONNECTICUT

Cos Cob is a derivation of the name of the Indian chief, Kosa Koba, whose tribe lived in the region. It is believed that his grave is located in the central part of the village.

BOWLEGS, OKLAHOMA

During the 1830's and 1840's, the Seminole Indians of Florida, having lost their final war to the white man, were removed from that state and sent to the Indian territory that is now part of Oklahoma.

A family of one of the early Seminole tribal leaders, Billy Bowlegs, settled in this section of Oklahoma, and the town was named in his honor. One can still visit the Bowlegs family burial grounds and also see a hand-painted portrait of Chief Billy Bowlegs hanging on the outer wall of the local post office.

SLEEPY EYE, MINNESOTA

Chief Sleepy Eyes (*Ish-Tak-Ha-Ba*) of the Lower Sisseton Dakota was a friend of the white settlers who started coming to this region in the 1860's. A beautiful lake and the town were named after this chief, whose grave and monument lie near the local railroad station.

TUSCALOOSA, ALABAMA

This region had been a favorite hunting ground of the Creek and Choctaw Indians. It is said that these tribes once played an Indian ball game to decide who would have hunting rights in the territory. This type of game, probably a kind of lacrosse, was a fierce affair, with hundreds of men competing to get a little hard ball into their respective goals.

Few white men dared go into this part of the wilderness. In 1540, Hernando de Soto and his Spanish warriors marched into the area and fought a bloody battle with the Indian tribes. Seven thousand Indians were killed, including the giant Chief Taskalusa. In the Choctaw and Creek tongues his name meant Black Warrior.

Hardship

LOST NATION, IOWA

According to legend, there was once a nation of Indians living in the wilds of what was to become the state of Iowa. They lived off the land, hunting in the brush and fishing in the lakes, and they were a happy people until one winter brought the fiercest cold weather and the deepest snows ever to hit this territory. Slowly, food ran out, and one by one the entire tribe perished from cold and hunger.

WACO, TEXAS

The town took its name from the Waco Indians, a tribe that lived in the area. The Wacos were originally forced to migrate to this region because of the pressure from other tribes to the north. Again in 1855 they were forced to go to the Brazos Indian Reservation in western Texas. Four years later the federal government made them take their last trek to the Indian Territory, in the south-central part of the United States (now Oklahoma).

Tribal Incidents

SHEBOYGAN, WISCONSIN

Sheboygan was an important area located on one of the three main trade routes used by settlers traveling from east to west. They usually followed the Erie Canal to Buffalo, New York, then took lake passenger boats to Sheboygan, where they transferred to overland wagon trains.

This land was called by the Potawatomi Indians *Shab-wa-wa-goning*, meaning "rumbling waters" or "waters disappearing underground."

An amusing legend, probably invented, tells us that the area got its name when an Indian chief, upon being told that his squaw gave birth to another *girl* papoose, exclaimed in exasperation: "She-boy-again!"

KALAMAZOO, MICHIGAN

In this fertile valley in Michigan lived the peace-loving Potawatomi tribe. The early settlers found them here in large numbers.

The Indians called this valley *Ke-ke-kala-kala-mazoo*, which means "where the water boils (or smokes) in the pot." It is believed that it got this name when an Indian brave bet he could run to the river and back before a pot of water could boil.

JUMPING BRANCH, WEST VIRGINIA

This region, according to old-timers, was thickly inhabited by Indians. It is said that when the Indians lived here, there was no other way to cross the local branch (stream) except by jumping. So they would jump back and forth. One day when one of them was trying to jump to the other side, his foot slipped on a muddy rock and he fell in and broke his neck. After that it was known as Jump-in-the-Branch, later shortened to Jumping Branch.

Landmarks

TEN SLEEP, WYOMING

The Indians often reckoned time by the number of days it took to go from one place to another. This village was ten days travel, or "sleeps," from several different points; Fort Laramie, Yellowstone, and the Indian agency in Stillwater County, Montana.

NINETY-SIX, SOUTH CAROLINA

Settled in 1730, this fortified settlement took its name from its mileage distance from Fort Prince George on the Keowee River. The first southern land battle of the American Revolution was fought here on November 19-21, 1775. A makeshift fort of fence rails and bales of straw was quickly thrown up by five hundred Patriots, who beat back an attack by a much larger force of Tories. The battle ended in a truce, men having been killed and wounded on both sides.

In June, 1781, the fort, held by Tories, was besieged by Americans under Nathanael Greene. The British relieved the fort in time, but later abandoned it.

BATON ROUGE, LOUISIANA

Legend says that French explorers, upon entering this area in 1719, saw a tall red cypress tree which was stripped of its bark. They gave the tree the name *le baton rouge*, meaning "the red stick." They later found out that "the red stick" marked the boundary between the lands of the Huma and Bayogoula Indians.

Since that time, seven different nations have flown their flags over Baton Rouge—France, England, Spain, Louisiana, the Florida Republic, the Confederate States, and the United States.

Communication

SIGNAL HILL, CALIFORNIA

The local Indians used this high hill to communicate with their neighbors. They built signal fires on it to send messages to tribes living on Santa Catalina Island, twenty-six miles away, which was much faster and safer than paddling across the San Pedro Channel to deliver the news in person.

When Spaniards set up a mission in the area, they used the hill as a signal station to warn their people of enemy attacks. Similarly, smugglers and pirates used it to tell their men at sea about ships that were loaded with gold, silver, and other valuable cargo.

PAINT ROCK, TEXAS

On the Limestone cliffs bordering the Concho River, there are Indian paintings showing how the tribes of yesteryear lived. These pictographs range from the Indians of prehistoric days to the Comanches, a tribe that hunted in this area until the beginning of the twentieth century.

Sports

BALLGROUND, MISSISSIPPI

Fifteen miles north of Vicksburg lies the town of Ballground, an old Indian name derived from four Indian mounds resembling large balls. Three are still standing.

The mounds were used as Indian burial grounds, with the area below them as a sports arena where several tribes—Choctaw, Chickasaw, and Yazoo—competed against each other. The tribal chiefs used the mounds as viewing stands to cheer on the participants.

NAMES FROM OTHER COUNTRIES

America is a land of immigrants who came to these shores to seek a brighter future. For many it was difficult to give up forever the land of their ancestors—a land they still had fond memories of. They thus kept a piece of their old countries by giving their new homes similar names.

Other reasons—geographical similarities or inspiration from a historic event—have also prompted Americans to give their towns foreign names. This is one of the many ways that the Old and New Worlds are tied to each other.

Named by New Immigrants

NEW SWEDEN, MAINE

On July 23, 1870, a group of wagons carrying fifty-one settlers from Sweden stopped in a wilderness in Maine that was destined to become New Sweden. These settlers, handpicked in Sweden for their pioneering venture by William Thomas, were thrifty, extremely honest, and quite religious. Together, they built cabin homes, cut forest timber, and planted crops. In a short time they built a school and set up two mills which produced the famous New Sweden shingles. When it was necessary, wives worked alongside their husbands clearing forests, planting, and harvesting. They style of life also called for abstinence from alcohol, a habit that has continued in New Sweden to this day.

NEW GERMANY, MINNESOTA

Early settlers who came here from Germany wrote back telling about the wonderful black soil, excellent growing conditions, and similarity to their former country. Their European relatives suggested that they name their pioneer home New Germany.

In the beginning, most of the people spoke German and conducted services in their mother tongue. Gradually German was displaced by English.

Historical Note: As a result of the conflict with Germany during World War I, a number of American towns with German names changed them for patriotic reasons or because of anti-German feeling. New Germany became Motordale, reverting to New Germany again after the war ended. The citizens of Brandenburg, Texas, renamed their town Old Glory in 1917, for the American flag. Germantown, Texas, became Schroeder, honoring a young soldier, P. W. Schroeder, who was killed in battle. Germantown, California, was changed to Artois in 1918, for a region in northern France. Potsdam, Missouri, originally named for Frederick the Great's city, was changed to Pershing in 1921, in honor of the World War I hero. The people in Germantown, Kansas, renamed their home Mercier, in honor of Cardinal D. J. Mercier, spokesman for the oppressed people of Belgium during the German occupation of that nation. His pastoral letters were a public protest to the invasion of the German armies.

HOLLAND, MICHIGAN

On a September morning in 1846, sixty Dutch men, women, and children got ready to leave Rotterdam, the Netherlands, for America. Lack of economic opportunities and religious differences at home made them willing to endure the forty-seven-day voyage across the Atlantic. Soon after they arrived, they were joined by hundreds of other Hollanders who wanted to be part of the planned city that was being created by the Reverend Albertus Van Raalte.

Their first summer was grueling, with insufficient shelter and diseases like malaria and dysentery widespread. It was so bad that the dead were hastily wrapped in sheets and buried under trees because there weren't enough healthy men to make coffins. But the Hollanders overcame this scourge, and went courageously on to create a healthy and happy community.

Every year in May, Holland holds a Dutch tulip festival, complete with national costume and dancing in *klompen*—wooden shoes—to commemorate its founding.

BELGIUM, WISCONSIN

In 1845 twelve families settled in this region, which was then part of the Northwest Territory. When Wisconsin became a state in 1848, the area was divided into townships. The twelve families called their town Belgium because all of them came from either Belgium or Luxembourg.

MOSCOW, IDAHO

This city went through a series of names before it settled on the present one in 1887. Originally it was called Hogs Heaven, a name which the town's ladies insisted on changing. It was known as Paradise until its first postmaster, a Russian immigrant, decided to call it Moscow.

SHAMROCK, TEXAS

Shamrock was first established as a post office in 1890 at the dugout home of George Nichols, an Irish sheep rancher. Nowadays, the town has an annual St. Patrick's Day celebration with real shamrocks and colleens competing on floats for the title of Miss Irish Rose.

LONDON BRIDGE, VIRGINIA

Among the first settlers here was a family named Lands, who had previously lived on London Bridge in England. This famous span over the Thames River had contained stores and residential apartments before the fire of 1688.

London Bridge was merged with Virginia Beach in 1963.

NEW HOLLAND, PENNSYLVANIA

Many immigrants from Germany and other areas of northern Europe took refuge in Holland before they embarked for the New World. The settlers in New Holland paid tribute to the hospitality and friendliness of the Dutch by naming the town in their honor.

NEW MADRID, MISSOURI

This area was part of the Louisiana Purchase, bought from France in 1803. Prior to this, it had belonged to Spain. Spanish authorities had, during the time of their rule, granted a parcel of land to Colonel George Morgan. The enterprising Morgan then brought settlers from Pennsylvania to establish a city on the Mississippi called New Madrid. The town was subject to a famous and devastating earthquake in 1811.

AMSTERDAM, OHIO

The town was laid out in 1823 by a Dutchman, David Johnson, who still had fond memories of his native Amsterdam.

STATEN ISLAND, NEW YORK

This name was derived from the States General, the legislative body that governed the Netherlands from the fifteenth century to the end of the eighteenth. In Dutch, the name is Staten-General.

Staten Island was the site of the only peace conference that tried to bring an early end to the American Revolution. On September 11, 1776, two months after the issuance of the Declaration of Independence, the two sides met at the Billopp house near Tottenville. Benjamin Franklin, John Adams, and Edward Rutledge represented the American side, and Admiral Lord Howe and his secretary, Henry Strachey, served as delegates for the British government. The conference came to nothing, however, because the American representatives refused to consider any terms that did not include independence.

Seven years later, Franklin, Adams, and Strachey were present at a second meeting in Paris, during which England signed a peace treaty recognizing the new nation.

LEWES, DELAWARE

Lewes, historically a place that was raided by pirates and bombarded by the British, is the first town of the first state. William Penn, the English Quaker, in whose territory Delaware was originally included, named the town after Lewes, located in Sussex, England.

MARIETTA, OHIO

On April 7, 1788, Marietta was founded by an entourage of forty-seven Revolutionary officers, soldiers, and private citizens who had traveled down the Ohio River from Pittsburgh. It was named for Queen Marie Antoinette of France, in appreciation for France's aid during the American Revolution.

On display in the town is a small bell, a gift from the Queen. It bears her personal heraldic device.

At the time the town was founded, the Ohio Land Company offered the Queen a square of land, which is now the famous Mound Cemetery.

PARIS, TEXAS

Settlers permanently established their community here in 1836. At that time, a French workman prevailed upon his boss, a wealthy landowner, to name the town after his beloved place of birth, Paris, France.

This northeastern Texas town has also been the home of some notorious outlaws. Frank James, after his gunslinging days, worked here in a dry-goods store on the downtown plaza. And the bandit queen, Belle Starr, spent a week in the Paris jail.

COVENTRY, VERMONT .

Coventry was founded November 4, 1780, by Major Elias Buell and fifty-nine others. Since Buell had been the principal agent in procuring the charter, he was given the right to name the new town. Being a native and former resident of Coventry, Connecticut, Buell named it Coventry.

Coventry, Connecticut, was named in 1711 for the city in central Warwickshire, England, of that name. The original Coventry is most famous for the legendary naked ride of Lady Godiva through the streets, in protest against her husband's taxes. The epithet "sent to Coventry" comes from the English Civil War (1642–1649), when Royalist prisoners were sent to Coventry for safekeeping.

DOVER, DELAWARE

William Penn, having acquired this land from the Duke of York, visited the area in 1683. Shortly afterward he issued a warrant stating how he wanted the town plotted, detailing such specifics as the width of streets and the location of the jail and the courthouse. Dover was finally laid out in 1717, incorporating many of Penn's original specifications.

It is said that he chose the name Dover in honor of Dover in Kent County, England, a place he was fond of.

Important Events

MEXICO, MAINE

From 1809 to 1815, Mexicans, influenced by the success of the American and French Revolutions, struggled with their Spanish overlords. This inspired the people in the little settlement of Holmanstown to rename their community Mexico in honor of their courageous North American brothers.

PERU, MAINE

This is another Maine town named in honor of a Latin American neighbor. Peru, Maine, received its name in 1821, the year that the Peruvian people won their freedom from Spanish rule.

SANTA FE, NEW MEXICO

Santa Fe (meaning "Holy Faith") was probably named for the same city in Andalusia, Spain. This community was founded and named by Ferdinand and Isabella during their final conquest of the Moors in 1492. Carrying over such names to the New World was a common practice for the conquistadors. There are Santa Fes in Argentina, Bolivia, Brazil, Cuba, the Philippines, and the Galapagos Islands.

Santa Fe is the capital of New Mexico and the oldest European community west of the Mississippi River.

COPENHAGEN, NEW YORK

Living side by side, in this upstate New York region, were British sympathizers (Federalists) and British haters (Republicans). Their running feud flared up when news came in 1807 that an English fleet had bombarded

Copenhagen in time of technical peace. The townspeople immediately called a meeting in which they decided to rename the town Copenhagen as an act of ridicule directed against the British and their Federalist supporters.

CANTON, OHIO

In Baltimore, Captain John O'Donnell, an Irish trader, bought a plantation naming it the Canton Estate. The name commemorated his carrying the first cargo to arrive in Baltimore from Canton, China.

Shortly after O'Donnell's death the town was named in his honor by Bezaleel Wells, a surveyor from Steubenville who had grown very fond of the old sea captain. Wells had large landholdings in the area that he had bought from a white man who had inherited it from a Delaware Indian.

EGYPT, TEXAS

The name "Egypt" was given to this farming community when it supplied corn to other settlements during a terrible drought. The Bible-reading people of the area remembered the role Joseph played in getting the Pharaoh of Egypt to store up his grain as a precaution against periods of drought.

Whims

CEYLON, MINNESOTA

The town had been called Tenhassen ("where the sugar maples grow"), but when a post office came, the authorities asked for a new name. The residents met to discuss the situation in the local grocery store, and while the debate raged, one of them spotted a can of Ceylon tea on the shelf. He suggested the "Ceylon" name and it was accepted.

CHINA, MAINE

Japheth C. Washburn, a representative in the Massachusetts legislature, named this town in 1818. This was the title of one of his favorite hymns and, at the time, the only such name in the United States. Today there is also a China in Texas and two Chinas in Mexico.

NORWAY, MICHIGAN

Originally called Ingolsdorf, this town's name was changed to Norway in 1891 because of the large number of Norway pines in the area. Ironically, there were few Norwegians in the area, the population being mainly English, Italian, Polish, and Swedish.

ATHENS, ALABAMA

It is believed that the early settlers here had a great love for culture, and hoped that their town would be as cultured as ancient Athens in Greece.

Similarity in Topography

CAIRO, ILLINOIS

This city (pronounced *kay*-row) was so named because of its many likenesses to Cairo, the capital of Egypt. It is built on a low-lying delta formed by the Ohio River, much like the Egyptian Cairo on the Nile.

There are also other towns up and down the Mississippi River that are named after Egyptian cities—Karnak, Dongola, and Thebes in Illinois, and Memphis in Tennessee. Because of this, southern Illinois became known as Little Egypt.

ODESSA, DELAWARE

The Appoquinimink, a small tidal creek that wanders through the marshes at the edge of this town, helped make Odessa a riverport in early American history. From this waterway flat-bottom open boats, called shallops, were used by the early inhabitants to trade with larger boats on the Delaware River, approximately three miles away.

A number of granaries were situated along the riverfront near a tall bridge that Edmund Cantwell built across the Appoquinimink in the middle of the seventeenth century. Large amounts of grain were shipped from Cantwell's Bridge—the first name of the town—to Philadelphia, New York, and other areas.

In 1855, hoping to rival the huge grain port of Odessa, Russia, the people decided to change their town name to Odessa. Soon after, however, a new railroad, laid three miles west of Odessa, deprived this pretty little Quaker town of its river traffic. Thereafter, both its commerce and its population rapidly decreased.

ODESSA, TEXAS

This was one of the many areas in the United States built with the labor of foreign workers. In this case, Russian railroad men, toiling on this section of the Texas and Pacific Railroad line, said that the wide, flat prairies reminded them of the steppes (grassy plains) of Odessa in the Ukraine.

EGYPT, MISSISSIPPI

This section of Mississippi was so fertile and so rich in nitrogen that excessive herbaceous growth prevented the planting of cotton—the common crop of the region. Thus, the farmers planted corn. In 1858, Colonel Charles Gates, aware of the biblical reference to Egypt as a "land of corn," gave the name to the locale, a station on the Mobile and Ohio Railroad. (The "corn" referred to in the Bible was probably wheat, since corn was not known in the Old World.)

ITALY, TEXAS

While traveling in Italy, the first postmaster of this settlement saw a great similarity between the climate and landscape of that country and of his homeland. When the time came for the town to have a name, he suggested "Sunny Italy" to the postal service. They cut it down to "Italy," which became the name of the post office and then the town. At that time there were no Italians living here, and even today, there are probably no more than two or three families of Italian ancestry residing in Italy, Texas.

The townspeople, in the 1930's, were so infuriated by Mussolini's invasion of Ethiopia that they cabled the dictator a petition of protest.

POLAND, NEW YORK

More than one hundred years ago the name of this village in Herkimer County was changed because—like Poland in Europe—it was situated to the west of Russia, a nearby town.

ROME, GEORGIA

Several men who stopped to rest and feed their horses in this area decided that it would be an ideal location for a town because of the abundance of water. Later, they got together and drew names from a hat to decide what to call their envisioned town. Rome was selected, a choice submitted by D. R. Mitchell because he noticed that the site was located on seven hills, like the Eternal City.

DUNKIRK, NEW YORK

Elisha Jenkins, a land-company agent for the western part of New York, saw a great resemblance between the Lake Erie bay of this area and the port of Dunkerque, France, where he had worked for many years. With his company's approval, Jenkins named the local village Dunkirk.

Dunkerque is perhaps best known for the heroic last stand made there by British and French troops in May, 1940, and their evacuation by a motley fleet of British, French, Dutch, and Belgian vessels of every size from ferryboat to private yacht.

But there are other, happier memories concerned with this town and its American namesake. At the close of World War I, the pastor of Dunkerque cathedral wrote an appeal to its sister city in America to help rebuild what the German bombardment had destroyed. Dunkirk, New York, immediately sent a large sum of money. During World War II, the mayor of this New York town sent a heartfelt message of encouragement to the mayor of Dunkerque, saying "Help is on the way. Victory is near." When the war was over, the people of Dunkirk once again pitched in and raised more than $200,000 worth of goods to help their friends in the war-torn French city across the ocean.

CLASSICAL NAMES

Thousands of American town names were taken from ancient Greek and Roman words, people, places, and myths. The name—of a Roman general or a Greek philosopher, of a Greek or Roman god—was often chosen indiscriminately, for no rhyme or reason. Sometimes the classical name was inspired by a topographical feature of the area, or a fond hope of the inhabitants, or an event that occurred in the vicinity.

At one time classical names were in high fashion. The neoclassical period began in France in 1789, as a result of the French Revolution, when the French were discarding all remnants of the Old Regime. People copied ancient Greek, Roman, and Egyptian models instead—for clothing, architecture, furniture, and names. This classical fad spread throughout Europe and into the impressionable United States. Thomas Jefferson, among others, thought highly of many aspects of Roman architecture, and used it in his designs for the Virginia capitol and for the circular library at the University of Virginia.

Thus, hardworking, plain-speaking people in many settlements throughout the country chose very elegant-sounding names for their towns.

Ancient Cities, Towns, and Districts

ATHENS

There are towns named Athens in Alabama, Florida, Georgia, Illinois, Kentucky, Louisiana, Maine, Michigan, New York, Ohio, Oregon, Tennessee, Texas, West Virginia, and Wisconsin.

121

The city in Georgia is the largest in population of all the Athens places named in the United States, with only Ohio's Athens County surpassing it.

The Georgia Athens was originally called Cedar Shoals, taking on its present name in 1806. Twenty years later the town boasted of having "583 free people, 16 four-wheeled carriages and 16 widows."

It is believed that the early settlers of Athens, Georgia, had a great love for culture, and hoped that their town would be as cultured as ancient Athens had been.

ARCADIA

There are towns named Arcadia in California, Florida, Iowa, Kansas, Louisiana, Michigan, Missouri, Nebraska, Oklahoma, Pennsylvania, Texas, and Wisconsin.

Arcadia was a mountainous pastoral region in central Peloponnesus, Greece.

Arcadia, Louisiana, according to Eva Grace Sutton, a local resident, "is an area of high hills and deep valleys, and at the time it was named, it was one of giant trees with no underbrush. My great grandfather, Shadrach P. Sutton, rode into the region on horseback. When he saw the area, being a student of Greek, he was reminded of the Arcadia of ancient Greece, which was a mountainous district noted for the contented simplicity of its people. So—he named the town Arcadia.

CORINTH

There are towns named Corinth in Georgia, Kentucky, Mississippi, New York, Texas, Vermont, and West Virginia.

Corinth was a city of ancient Greece on the Gulf of Corinth.

Corinth, Mississippi, was the site of a Civil War clash, October 3–4, 1862.

DELPHI

There are towns named Delphi in Alaska, Indiana, and Montana.

This town in ancient Greece was the seat of an oracle of Apollo.

Delphi, Alaska, was originally called Carroll, in honor of the last surviving signer of the Declaration of Independence, Maryland's Charles Caroll of Carrollton. He died in 1832 at the age of ninety-five.

In time, conflict arose over the name, and a new one was demanded by a number of the townspeople. A meeting was held at which General Samuel Milroy, a founder of the town, was asked to select a name. General Milroy, an avid reader of ancient history, wrote three historical names on slips of paper, putting them into a hat. Delphi was chosen.

HERCULANEUM

Herculaneum, Missouri, was named after the ancient city that was destroyed with Pompeii when Mount Vesuvius erupted in A.D. 79.

This place in Missouri was named by Moses Austin in 1808, a founder of the town, in memory of the beautiful ancient city. Moses was the father of Stephen Fuller Austin, who after Moses' death carried out his father's plans for colonizing Texas and was the earliest leader of that state's independence movement. Austin, the capital, is named for him.

KARNAK

Karnak, Illinois, is named after a village on the Nile River in east-central Egypt, occupying the northern part of ancient Thebes. (The southern part is called Luxor.)

There is also a Karnack, Texas, which is located a short distance from Carthage, Texas.

MACEDONIA

There are towns named Macedonia in Connecticut, Illinois, Iowa, and Ohio.

Macedonia was an ancient kingdom, north of Greece. It gained great power under Alexander the Great, who ruled it from 336 to 323 B.C.

The towns in Ohio and Iowa adopted their names in a very similar manner. In Iowa the first religious service in the area was conducted by the Mormons, who were going west to Salt Lake City. The service, which was held in a gristmill along the Nishnabotna River, began with a sermon from Acts 16:9:

"And a vision appeared to Paul in the night; there stood a man of Macedonia and prayed him, saying, Come over into Macedonia, and help us."

A community, which settled around the mill, later recalled the sermon and gave the name "Macedonia" to their town.

In Ohio, the first settlers wanted a clergyman but were too poor to hire one. In their need they called upon the seminary in nearby Hudson, Ohio, to come to their settlement and conduct services. The student ministers looked upon these requests as a "Macedonian call." This inspired the community to give this name to their home.

MARATHON

There are towns named Marathon in Florida, Iowa, New York, Texas, and Wisconsin.

Marathon is a plain in eastern Attica, Greece, where the Persians were defeated by the Athenians and Plateaeans in 490 B.C.

Marathon, in the heart of the Florida Keys, is part of a dream that Henry M. Flagler, the pioneer builder of the east coast of Florida, made into a reality in the early part of the twentieth century.

In 1904 he decided to extend a railroad from mainland Florida to Key West. It was a Herculean task calling for fills, viaducts, and bridges strong enough to withstand fierce tropical storms. The crews had to work in the Everglades, fighting hurricanes and unpredictable currents. The pace was swift, in an attempt to complete the railroad during the ebbing life of the aged Mr. Flagler.

According to legend, a workman is supposed to have exclaimed: "Gee, this is getting to be a regular marathon!" The name stuck, and the area where the construction crew was working became known as Marathon, Florida.

In Texas, a sea captain suggested the name because the area reminded him of Marathon, Greece.

MEMPHIS

There are towns named Memphis in Florida, Indiana, Michigan, Missouri, Nebraska, Tennessee, and Texas.

The city in Tennessee was tied to the Mississippi River, as was Memphis, the capital of ancient Egypt, part and parcel of the Nile. Andrew Jackson helped prepare for the establishment of this community by working out a settlement with the Chickasaw Indians in 1818. He then met with John Overton and James Winchester, who had drawn up specific plans for "Memphis"—a name that is said to have been chosen by Jackson.

ROME

There are towns named Rome in Georgia, Illinois, Indiana, Kansas, Kentucky, Massachusetts, Mississippi, Missouri, New York, Oregon, Pennsylvania, and Tennessee.

In Georgia, several men who stopped to rest and feed their horses in this area decided that it would be an ideal location for a town because of the abundance of water. Later, they got together and drew names from a hat to decide what to call their envisioned town. Rome was selected, a choice submitted by D. R. Mitchell because he noticed that the sight was located on seven hills, like ancient Rome.

SPARTA

There are towns named Sparta in Georgia, Illinois, Kentucky, Michigan, Missouri, New Jersey, North Carolina, Tennessee, and Wisconsin, as well as Spartanburg in Indiana and South Carolina.

The ancient Greek city-state was known for the military prowess of its citizens, and hence it appealed to many town namers who admired courage and fortitude.

In 1809 Sparta, Tennessee, was named and designated as the new county seat, chosen by the townspeople to be on the east side of the Calf Killer River.

Spartanburg, South Carolina, got its name from a Revolutionary War band of militia called the Spartan Rifles, who made this area their headquarters. The suffix "burg" was added by German-speaking settlers.

SYRACUSE

There are towns named Syracuse in Indiana, Kentucky, Missouri, Nebraska, New York, Ohio, and Utah.

Syracuse was a city on the east coast of Sicily, settled in the eighth century B.C. by Greeks from Corinth. Its successful repulsion of an attempted Athenian invasion in 415–413 B.C. led ultimately to Athens' defeat in the Peloponnesian War.

The city in New York State was named in an interesting way.

In 1820, a young lawyer, John Wilkinson, had been appointed to a committee to help select a new name for the town of Corinth, New York. One that intrigued him was "Syracuse," after an ancient city in Sicily. He saw many similarities between it and his own town. He associated the legendary fountain of ancient Syracuse with the fresh water of Onondaga Lake, both being about the same size and both having springs of fresh water and saltwater along their banks. Also, to the north of each community was a village called Salina, and the two cities were located at halfway points on major travel routes. Moreover, the settlers of ancient Syracuse had emigrated from ancient Corinth in Greece.

This information was presented to the committee, which unanimously agreed to give the name "Syracuse" to the new post office and town.

THEBES

Thebes was a city in ancient Greece. The Thebans destroyed the power of Sparta in 371 B.C. and were defeated in turn by the Macedonians in 338 B.C. Two years later, when the Thebans revolted, Alexander the Great seized the city and enslaved its population.

Thebes, Illinois, lies in Alexander County.

TROY

There are towns named Troy in Alabama, Idaho, Illinois, Indiana, Iowa, Kansas, Maine, Michigan, Mississippi, Missouri, Montana, New Hampshire, New York, North Carolina, Ohio, Oklahoma, Oregon, Pennsylvania, South Carolina, Tennessee, Utah, Virginia, and West Virginia.

Troy, a city in Asia Minor, was the site of the Trojan War, a ten-year conflict of Greeks against Trojans, which ended with the burning of Troy.

Troy, New York, lies at the head of navigation on the Hudson River. It is famous, however, not for its classical name but for an inspector of goods supplied to the government during the War of 1812, Samuel Wilson. Goods that passed inspection were stamped "U.S.," which locals identified with Wilson's nickname, "Uncle Sam." In time, the United States government inherited the nickname.

CRETE

There are towns named Crete in Illinois, Nebraska, and North Dakota.

Crete is an island lying off the southeast coast of Greece in the Mediterranean Sea.

In 1843, Willard Irwyn Wood, founder of Crete, Illinois, was appointed the town's first postmaster and asked to choose a name. Mr. Wood, a religious man, opened the New Testament at random, pointed his finger to a name, and chose it for the post office. His finger had rested on the history of Paul's journey as a prisoner to Rome, as related in Acts 27:7,12,13, which mentioned the island Crete.

Jesse C. Bickle was the first white settler to inhabit the area of Crete, Nebraska. In 1863 he built a two-room cabin on the banks of the Blue River, the site taking that name. The post office was called Crete, in honor of Crete, Illinois, Mrs. Bickle's hometown. In time, the name Crete dominated, replacing Blue River.

On June 12, 1871, when the first train came to Crete on the newly constructed railroad line, its passengers saw a typical frontier village: there were nine saloons, but no schools or churches.

Islands, Mountains, and Shrines

PATMOS

There are towns named Patmos in Arkansas and Ohio.

The original Patmos is one of the Dodecanese Islands—a group of Greek Islands in the Aegean Sea between Turkey and Crete. John the Evangelist was exiled to Patmos in 95 A.D., and he is supposed to have written the Apocalypse there.

RHODES

There are towns named Rhodes in Iowa and Michigan.

The capital and largest of the Dodecanese Islands, Rhodes, derives its name from the word for "rose," *rhodon*.

OLYMPIA

There are towns named Olympia in California, Kentucky, and Washington.

Ancient Olympia was a plain of Elis in the northwestern Peloponnesus, where the original Olympic games were held in honor of Zeus, the Olympic god. Mount Olympus is the highest mountain in Greece and in Greek mythology was the abode of the Greek gods.

Olympia, Washington, was originally called Smithter, a combination of the names of the first two settlers—Edmund Sylvester and L. L. Smith. It was changed to Smithfield and later named for the nearby Olympic Mountains.

The mountains, which lie to the north of the city, were given their name, it is said, by Captain John Meares in 1788. Quite impressed with the sight of the mountain peak he saw when he sailed his British frigate *Merryweather* into the area, Meares is quoted as having said: "If that be not the home where dwell the gods, it is certainly beautiful enough to be and I therefore will call it Olympus."

PARTHENON

Parthenon, Arkansas, is named for the famous temple to Athena built on the Acropolis at Athens in the fifth century B.C. The name is derived from *parthenos*, the Greek word for "maiden." Athena was called the maiden goddess.

Greek Mythology

ACHILLES

There is an Achilles, Virginia, and an Achille, Oklahoma.

Achilles, the heroic warrior, was a leading figure in Homer's *Iliad*.

APOLLO

Apollo, Pennsylvania, is named for the god of the sun, prophecy, music, medicine, and poetry. His most famous temple was established at Delphi near Mount Parnassus, where priestesses gave advice and enigmatic prophecies to worshipers.

ARGO

There are towns named Argo in Alabama, Kentucky, and Texas, plus Argonia, Kansas, and Argos, Indiana.

Argos was the city of ancient Greece—perhaps the oldest—where Jason and his Argonauts came from.

Argo was the name of the ship in which Jason sailed in search of the

Golden Fleece. He and his men, with Medea's aid, stole the fleece of the golden ram from the king of Colchis.

ARGUS

There are towns named Argusville in New York and North Dakota.

The original Argus was a giant with a hundred eyes, who was slain by Hermes.

ATHENA

There are towns named Athena in Florida and Oregon.

Athena was the Greek goddess of wisdom and the arts. Her symbol is the owl.

CHARYBDIS

Near Charybdis, California, is the town of Scylla, California.

The original Charybdis was a whirlpool on the Italian side of the Strait of Messina. Opposite this was Scylla, a legendary female sea monster that ate sailors who escaped the danger of the whirlpool.

CLIO

There are towns named Clio in Alabama, California, Iowa, Michigan, and South Carolina.

The original Clio was the Greek muse of history.

Clio, Michigan, is said to have acquired its name by a fluke. Selected as the site of a railroad watering tank, the area was marked down in railroad code as CL-10. Settlers read the sign as Clio, and it was entered thus on the map.

GALATEA

There is a Galatea in California, and towns named Galatia in Ilinois and Kansas.

Pygmalion, king of Cyprus, fell in love with the ivory statue of a maiden that he had carved. Hearing his lovesick pleas, Aphrodite, the goddess of love and beauty, brought his creation, Galatea, to life.

HERCULES

Hercules, California, was named for the son of the god Zeus and Alcmene, a mortal woman. Hercules used his great strength to win immortality by completing the twelve tasks set forth by Hera, the sister and wife of Zeus.

HYGEIA

Mount Hygeia, Rhode Island, was named for the goddess of health, Hygeia, regarded as the daughter of Asclepius.

ITHACA

There are towns named Ithaca in Michigan, Nebraska, and New York.

The original Ithaca is an island of Greece, in the Ionian Sea, legendary home of Odysseus.

Simeon DeWitt, surveyor general of the state of New York, named the land that he owned Ithaca, because it was the main settlement in the town of Odysseus.

Ithaca, New York, is one of the many New York State towns that have classical names. At the turn of the century this section of the state was part of a military tract that had been laid out and surveyed into townships. Someone, apparently lacking names and having access to a classical dictionary, helped make New York the state endowed with the greatest number of classical Greek and Roman names.

Other New York places having classical names are as follows:

Argusville	Hannibal	Pharsalia
Athens	Homer	Philadelphia
Attica	Ilion	Phoenix
Brutus	Ionia	Phoenicia
Camillus	Lysander	Pomona
Carthage	Manlius	Rome
Cato	Marathon	Romulus
Cicero	Marcellus	Scipio
Cincinnatus	Medusa	Solon
Corfu	Minerva	Troy
Corinth	Minoa	Ulysses
Fabius	Ovid	Virgil

Roman Mythology

CERES

There are towns named Ceres in California, Nebraska, New York, and Virginia, plus Ceresco, Nebraska, and Ceredo, Kentucky.

Ceres was the Roman goddess of agriculture, and consequently many farming communities were attracted to her name.

JUNO

There are towns named Juno in Florida and Texas.

Juno was the principal goddess of the Pantheon, and the wife and sister of Jupiter. She was believed to be the patroness of marriage and the well-being of women.

JUPITER

Jupiter, Florida, was named after the supreme god of the Roman state, who was also called Jove.

Spanish explorers visiting this area in late 1555 found a tribe of Jeaga Indians who called themselves Jobes. This was pronounced by the Spaniards *Hoe-bay*, a name they gave to the local river. Two centuries later, in 1763, English settlers gave their own British pronunciation to the river and locale, calling it Jove. In referring to the area they often used the other name of this chief Roman god—Jupiter.

MARS

There are towns named Mars in Maine, North Carolina, and Pennsylvania.

Mars was the Roman god of war and the origin of our word "martial."

MINERVA

There are towns named Minerva in Kentucky, New York, Ohio, and Texas.

Minerva was the goddess of wisdom, invention, and the arts, the Roman counterpart of Athena.

NEPTUNE

There are towns named Neptune in New Jersey and Ohio, and there's a Neptune Beach in Florida.

Neptune was the Roman god of the sea.

PLUTO

Pluto, West Virginia, was named after the god of the dead and ruler of the underworld.

POMONA

There are towns named Pomona in California, Illinois, Kansas, Maryland, Missouri, New York, and North Carolina.

Pomona was the ancient Italian goddess of fruit trees, so the name was popular in orchard country.

ROMULUS

There are towns named Romulus in Michigan and New York.

According to legend, Romulus, the son of Mars, was abandoned as an infant along with his brother Remus, and left to die. Adopted and raised by a she-wolf, Romulus founded Rome in 753 B.C., becoming its first king.

VENUS

There are towns named Venus in Florida, Nebraska, Texas, and West Virginia.

Venus was the Roman goddess of love and beauty.

The settlers in Venus, Texas, chose the name because they thought the town and the surrounding countryside were as beautiful as the goddess and the bright star, Venus.

VESTA

There are towns named Vesta in Georgia, Minnesota, and Nebraska. There are also Vestaburg in Michigan and Pennsylvania; Vestal, in New York; Vestavia Hills, in Alabama; and Kalvesta, in Kansas.

Vesta was the goddess of the hearth. She was worshiped in a temple that contained the sacred fire, and this was tended constantly by the vestal virgins, maidens specially chosen from good families and dedicated to a life of chastity.

VULCAN

There are towns named Vulcan in Michigan and West Virginia.

Vulcan was the Roman god of fire and craftsmanship, especially metalworking, and it seemed a suitable name for a mining town.

ULYSSES

There are towns named Ulysses in Kansas, Kentucky, and Nebraska.

Ulysses is the Latin name for Odysseus, wily king of Ithaca and a leader of the Greeks in the Trojan War. Homer's *Odyssey* tells of his adventures and ten-year wanderings after the fall of Troy. Poseidon, god of the waters, earthquakes, and horses, had prevented Ulysses from returning to his home.

Most places named Ulysses are in honor of Ulysses S. Grant, Civil War general and President of the United States.

Other Mythologies

PHOENIX

There are towns named Phoenix in Arizona, Illinois, Louisiana, Maryland, Michigan, New York, and Oregon; plus Phoenixville, Pennsylvania.

An Egyptian myth tells of the five-hundred-year-old Phoenix bird which, having consumed itself by fire, rose from its own ashes, completely renewed.

THOR

Thor, Iowa, was named for Thor, the god of thunder in Norse mythology.

On this townsite, about a hundred years ago, a fierce argument over the naming of the town took place between Ole Willecksen, a Norwegian settler, and railroad authorities. Mr. Willeckesen wanted it named for his wife, a request that was totally unacceptable to the rail people. At one point in the discussion Willecksen said, "If we're going to fight like thunder, we might as well name it after the god of thunder, Thor!" The rail people liked the name and accepted it.

Greek and Roman Historical Names

PLATO

There are towns named Plato in Colorado, Minnesota, and Missouri.

Plato was a Greek philosopher and a disciple of Socrates. Originally known as Aristocles, he was nicknamed Plato (from *platys*, "broad") for his broad shoulders.

CAESAR

Caesar is a town in Mississippi, and Caesars Head is in North Carolina.

Caesar was the surname of eleven early Roman emperors and of the famous general and statesman Gaius Julius Caesar.

By extension, "caesar" came to mean "emperor." Both *Kaiser* and *Tsar* are derived from "caesar."

CATO

There are towns named Cato in Arkansas, Indiana, Missouri, and New York.

Marcus Porcius Cato was an early Roman statesman.

Cato, Missouri, was named by Christopher Snyder, the town's first postmaster. The post office, in the early 1900's, was located in Mr. Snyder's house.

CINCINNATUS

There are towns named Cincinnati in Iowa and Ohio.

Lucius Quinctius Cincinnatus was an early Roman general. Appointed dictator during a crisis, Cincinnatus was found plowing his own fields by the delegation bringing him the news. When the enemy was defeated, he returned to the farm and quietly resumed his plowing. To early Americans, Cincinnatus seemed an ideal model for their own simple republic and its volunteer militia.

CONSTANTINE

Constantine, Michigan, was named for the Roman Emperor Constantine the Great (Flavius Valerius Aurelius Constantinus), best known for his adoption of Christianity. He ruled from A.D. 306 to 337.

FABIUS

There are towns named Fabius in Alabama, New York, and West Virginia.

The Roman general Quintus Fabius Maximus defeated Hannibal in the second Punic War. Surnamed *Cunctator* ("the delayer"), Fabius avoided action with the Carthaginian leader until he had worn him out. Hence, Washington is known as the American Fabius, and the term "fabian" is used to denote caution or delay.

HANNIBAL

There are towns named Hannibal in Missouri, New York, Ohio, and Wisconsin.

The famous Carthaginian general is perhaps best known for his crossing the Alps with a detachment of war elephants in his train.

Hannibal, Missouri, was Mark Twain's home town and the fictional site of some of his best stories.

MANLIUS

There are towns named Manlius in Illinois and New York.

Marcus Manlius Capitolinus discovered a night attack on Rome by the

Gauls in 390 B.C. Awakened by the cackling of geese, he led the counterattack that saved the city.

MARCELLUS

There are towns named Marcellus in Michigan, New York, and Washington.

Marcellus was an opponent of Julius Caesar.

POMPEY

Pompey's Pillar, Montana, was named after Pompey (Gnaeus Pompeius Magnus), a Roman statesman, general, and rival of Julius Caesar.

SCIPIO

There are towns named Scipio in Indiana, Oklahoma, and Utah.

Scipio Africanus the Elder was a Roman general and victor in the second Punic War.

SENECA

There are towns named Seneca in Illinois, Kansas, Maryland, Missouri, Nebraska, Ohio, Oregon, Pennsylvania, South Carolina, South Dakota, and Wisconsin. There is also Seneca Falls, New York.

Lucius Annaeus Seneca was a Roman philosopher, political leader, and author of tragedies.

Seneca, Kansas, had its beginning in 1857, when J. B. Ingersoll staked it out. Originally called Castle Rock, it was changed to Seneca by the town company for either the Roman Seneca or for the North American Indians of that name.

Seneca, Illinois, was originally known as Crotty Town, for Jeremiah Crotty, a hardworking, enterprising, Irish-born settler who helped develop the area. However, in 1853 the Chicago, Rock Island and Pacific Railroad named its local station Seneca, and a decade later, the post office, previously called Crotty, was changed to Seneca. In time Seneca also became the name of the town.

SOLON

There are towns named Solon in Iowa, Maine, and New York.

Solon was an Athenian statesman and poet who was known for his legal reforms.

VIRGIL

There are towns named Virgil in Illinois, Kansas, New York, and South Dakota.

Aeneas, South Dakota, had a rough start. It was settled in 1882 and destroyed by a cyclone the same year. It was rebuilt in 1883 and named in admiration of the poet Publius Vergilius Maro. Virgil is usually regarded as Rome's finest poet. His masterpiece is the epic poem the *Aeneid*, which tells the adventures of the Trojan hero Aeneas after he escaped from Troy and wandered for seven years, before landing in Italy and founding Lavinium, the parent city of Rome.

Greek and Latin Words

ADELPHI

There are towns named Adelphi in North Dakota, Maryland, and Ohio.

The name is taken from the Greek word *adelphos*, "brother." In Ohio two brothers helped found the town.

ARTAS

Artas, South Dakota, is named after the Greek word for a "loaf of wheat bread," *artos*. This part of South Dakota is a wheat-growing region.

EUREKA

There are towns named Eureka in Alaska, California, Florida, Illinois, Kansas, Minnesota, Montana, Nevada, South Carolina, South Dakota, Texas, Utah, and Washington.

The name comes from the Greek word *eureka*, "I have found."

Archimedes, the Greek mathematician, is believed to have uttered this expression when he made an important scientific discovery in his bath. Seeing the water rise as he immersed himself, he hit upon the theory of displacement, which solved a problem that had been bothering him. He exclaimed: "Eureka!" ("I have found [it]!")

A number of the towns named above were mining locations—as one might expect.

LITHOPOLIS

In Greek, *lithos* is stone, and *polis* is city—hence, stone city. There is a local stone quarry in the area of Lithopolis, Ohio.

PHILADELPHIA

There are towns named Philadelphia in Mississippi, Missouri, New York, Pennsylvania, and Tennessee.

Philadelphia is a combination of two Greek words meaning "brotherly love."

There was also the ancient city of Philadelphia, which was a commercial center in Lydia, Asia Minor.

PHILOMATH

There are towns named Philomath in Georgia and Oregon; and there's a Philo in California and Illinois.

Math is from the Greek *mathein*, "to learn," and *philos* is "friend" — "friend of learning."

Philomath, Oregon, is the site of a college.

PONTA

Pons is "bridge" in Latin. The town of Ponta, Texas, is near two bridges.

POMARIA

Pomarius is a Latin adjective for "fruited." Pomaria, South Carolina, is a fruit-growing area.

RENOVO

In Latin *renovo* means "I make new again." Renovo, Pennsylvania, is a place where railroad repair shops were located.

RIVANNA

The name is derived from the Latin word for "small river." The town of Rivanna, Virginia, is located near the river.

ALPHA

There are towns named Alpha in California, Idaho, Illinois, Michigan, Ohio, and Oklahoma.

Alpha is the first letter in the Greek alphabet. Added to *beta*, the second letter, it gives us the word "alphabet."

OMEGA

There are towns named Omega in Georgia, Nebraska, and Ohio.

Omega is the twenty-fourth and last letter in the Greek alphabet. In Revelation 21:6, Jesus is quoted as saying to John: "I am Alpha and Omega, the beginning and the end."

DELTA

There are towns named Delta in Alabama, Colorado, Louisiana, Michigan, Missouri, Ohio, Pennsylvania, Texas, and Utah.

The Greek letter *delta* is written as a triangle. There are deltas— triangular alluvial deposits—at the mouths of rivers in such areas as Delta, Louisiana.

NEON

Several areas in Kentucky are named for rare gaseous elements that were discovered at the turn of the century: Neon (the new), Krypton (hidden), and Xena (stranger).

ARCANUM

There are towns named Arcanum in Ohio and Virginia.

The Latin word for a mystery or a secret, *arcanum* was the great secret of nature that the alchemists attempted to find.

CENTROPOLIS

There are towns named Centropolis in Kansas and Missouri.

The name comes from the Greek *kentron*, "center" of a circle, and *polis*, "city."

DEMOPOLIS

The name for this city in Alabama means "people city" or "city of the people," from the Greek *demos*—people or district.

NEOPOLIS

The name of Neopolis, Tennessee, comes from the Greek *neos*, "new."

MINNEAPOLIS

There are towns named Minneapolis in Kansas, Minnesota, and North Carolina.

In Minnesota the name was suggested by a Mr. Charles Hoag in 1852. It is a contraction of the Indian word *minnehaha*, "falling water," and the Greek word *polis*, "city."

THERMOPOLIS

In the late 1890's the town of Thermopolis, Wyoming, was named for the hot springs that are a natural feature of the region. The word "thermopolis," by definition, is composed of *thermos*, "heat," and *polis*, "city," and its literal meaning is thus "hot city."

Namesake Towns

ATTICA

There are towns named Attica in Indiana, Iowa, Kansas, New York, and Ohio.

Attica was a state in ancient Greece of which Athens was the center.

In 1829, the name Attica (Ohio) was suggested by Ezra Gilbert, a tavern owner, for his old hometown of Attica, New York.

A year later, Attica had its first schoolhouse, a one-room log cabin where Samuel Miller instructed a dozen pupils for a monthly salary of twelve dollars.

This little town of one thousand people takes pride in having been sort of a melting pot of nations, having had inhabitants from England, Scotland, Ireland, Norway, Canada, Greece, Austria, Russia, Germany, Italy, France, and Japan.

CARTHAGE

There are towns named Carthage in Arkansas, Illinois, Indiana, Kentucky, Maine, Mississippi, Missouri, New Mexico, New York, North Carolina, South Carolina, Tennessee, and Texas.

Carthage was founded by Phoenician settlers in the ninth century B.C. It became a city-state on the north coast of Africa and the base of a great sea power. Rome annexed the territory when it defeated the Carthaginians in the Punic Wars.

In Carthage, Mississippi, on July 31, 1834, the Board of Police selected the site and gave it the name. The choice was probably influenced by important settlers who had moved from Carthage, Tennessee.

CICERO

There are towns named Cicero in Illinois, Indiana, Kansas, and New York.

Marcus Tullius Cicero was a Roman orator, essayist, and statesman.

In 1857, the Clerk of Cook County, Illinois, posted a notice within this township asking that the people organize a government. At the forthcoming town meeting the name Cicero was chosen. It had been suggested by Augustus Porter, a former resident of Cicero, New York.

In Indiana, some say that Cicero Laughlin, a son of one of the surveyors, fell into the local creek, creating an incident that resulted in the town's being called Cicero.

GALLIPOLIS

Gallipolis, Ohio, known as the old French City, was founded in 1790 by five hundred French immigrants who had left their native country as a result of the French Revolution and been enticed to the unbroken wilderness by a fraudulent land scheme. Many of them grimly stuck it out, however, and the town survived.

In naming their new home they combined the Latin *Galli*, the ancient name of the French people, with the Greek *polis*, "city." Today local people pronounce it *Gal-uh-police*.

IONIA

There are towns named Ionia in Iowa, Kansas, Michigan, Missouri, and New York.

The original Ionia was an area on the Aegean coast of western Asia Minor.

In November 1832, sixty-two settlers from New York traveled on the Erie Canal to Detroit, then across country by oxcart and riverboat to the Michigan region. They arrived, seven months later, in June, immediately buying the wigwams and crops of the local Indians. The site was soon named Ionia, the same name as a town in the geographical area in New York State from which the settlers had migrated.

OVID

There are towns named Ovid in Colorado, Idaho, Michigan, and New York.

Publius Ovidius Naso was a Roman poet.

The site in Michigan was named by settlers who emigrated from Ovid (later Seneca Falls), New York in July 1836.

Local People

ALEXANDRIA

There are towns named Alexandria in Indiana, Kentucky, Louisiana, Minnesota, Missouri, Nebraska, New Hampshire, Ohio, Pennsylvania, South Dakota, Tennessee, and Virginia, as well as Alexandria Bay, New York.

Alexandria was a city of Egypt, on the Mediterranean coast, founded by Alexander the Great in 332 B.C. The city was known for its school of Hellenistic philosophy, literature, and science.

Two pioneer brothers, Alexander and William Kinkead, settled in the Minnesota region in 1858. The town later took the name of the older brother.

AUGUSTA

There are towns named Augusta in Arkansas, Georgia, Illinois, Kansas, Kentucky, Maine, Michigan, Missouri, Montana, New Jersey, Ohio, West Virginia, Wisconsin, and Virginia, and there's an Augustus in Texas.

"Augustus" was a title of the Roman emperors, being equivalent to "Imperial Majesty." By extension, "Augusta" was applied to the wife, mother, daughter, or sister of the emperor.

The town in Kansas was originally called Fontanella by a group that came from Topeka in 1858. The following year they were driven out by the local Indians. After the Civil War and a 1868 peace treaty with the Osage Indians, two men, Shamleffer and James, bought the old claim for forty dollars and built a trading post. Mr. James became the first postmaster in 1869, giving the station and the town the name of his wife, Augusta.

HOMER

There are towns named Homer in Alaska, Georgia, Illinois, Louisiana, Michigan, Nebraska, and New York.

Homer was the greatest of the Greek poets, author of the epics *The Iliad* and *Odyssey*.

The town in Alaska was named for Homer Pennock, manager of the

Michigan Mining Company. His company supplied coal, transported by railway, to coal-burning steamers, which put into port for refueling. This ended about the time of World War I.

One can still see mementos—locomotive wheels, for instance—from that era, in front of the Salty Dawg Saloon.

OCTAVIA

There are towns named Octavia in Nebraska and Oklahoma.

Gaius Octavius was the grand-nephew and adopted son of Julius Caesar, the founder of the Roman Empire.

The village in eastern Nebraska was laid out in 1857 and named in honor of Octavia Speltz, wife of an influential local farmer.

PEOPLE'S NAMES

Innumerable towns throughout the United States have been named for people—all kinds of people, those historically famous, those prominent in an area, those who were town founders. It is a tribute to the diversity and democracy of America that it could have towns in the same state (Texas) named for an oil driller (McCamey) and for an English duke (Wellington).

Historically Famous

NAPOLEONVILLE, LOUISIANA

According to the town clerk, Napoleon Bonaparte's chief gunner at Waterloo, a man named Dominique, named the town after the Emperor. Following Napoleon's exile on the island of St. Helena, Dominique escaped from France to serve as the chief gunner for the pirate Jean Laffite. Dominique got to know this part of Louisiana well because the pirate ships often sailed up the Bayou Lafourche. Dominique came here to live after Laffite had moved away, and, being a powerful force in the town, got the people to name it for his beloved leader, Napoleon.

POCAHONTAS, VIRGINIA

The town was named for the Indian princess, born in 1595 and daughter of the Algonkian chief Powhatan. According to John Smith's own narrative, twelve-year-old Pocahontas saved his life. Captured and sentenced to

145

death by her father, he was led up to some rocks and his head placed on them, while warriors stood poised with clubs to bash his brains out. Pocahontas darted up, laid her head on the prisoner's, and pleaded with her father to release him. He did so.

"Pocahontas" was actually only a nickname meaning "frolicsome." The girl's formal name was Matooka. She became a Christian in later years, married a planter named John Rolfe, and sailed with her husband to England, where she was welcomed by the King and Queen. She became ill during her stay and died on March 29, 1617, at the age of twenty-two.

Many families of Virginia trace their descent from the one son, Thomas, whom she left in America.

TOWNSHEND, VERMONT

The town was named, in the eighteenth century, for Charles Townshend, a powerful English politician. He began his career in the House of Commons in 1747, rapidly rising through several ministries to become the all-important Chancellor of the Exchequer.

As chancellor he was responsible for several revenue-raising acts that enraged the colonists. The most famous of these was the Townshend Duty Act, which laid a tax on the importation of painters' colors, red and white lead, glass, paper, and tea. The acts were intensely resented and proved to be an effective catalyst in mustering colonial resistance to Parliament's rule.

Charles Townshend, who had never been to America, would never fully know the hornet's nest he had created, for he died four months after this tax bill became law.

WELLINGTON, TEXAS

Before 1890 this spread, owned by Baron Tweedmouth and the Earl of Aberdeen, was called the Nobility Ranch by Texas cowboys. It was later named for the Duke of Wellington, as was the town that grew up there.

OLD HICKORY, TENNESSEE

This town was named for Andrew "Old Hickory" Jackson, seventh President of the United States. In 1792 Jackson bought 330 acres of land here to build his first home for his wife. His other famous mansion, The Hermitage, is situated just three miles east of Old Hickory.

JACKSON COUNTY, MISSOURI

When Missouri came into the Union in 1821, it was the practice to designate counties and county seats. Jackson County was named after Andrew Jackson, and the county seat given his slogan "Independence." Clay County was named after Henry Clay, and its county seat given his slogan, "Liberty."

HILO, HAWAII

In Hawaiian, the word "hilo" means "twisted, braided, spun, thread-like, the first night of the new moon—crescent, curving." Perhaps this is how Hilo, the Polynesian navigator, who was said to have a crooked leg, got his nickname. Hilo, Hawaii, which bears his name, was one of the many parts of the Pacific Ocean he is said to have sailed to.

BOERNE, TEXAS

In 1851, German settlers established this community and named it in honor of a man they greatly admired—Karl Ludwig Boerne, a famous journalist who was exiled from his home because of his liberal writings. Boerne, who sympathized with the poor and oppressed, had died fourteen years earlier.

The German language and culture still play an important role in the lives of the people of Boerne, and every June they celebrate a festival they call a Berges Fest (the local spelling) complete with *oom-pah* music and native German costumes.

KING AND QUEEN, VIRGINIA

The county was formed in 1691 from New Kent and named in honor of King William III and Queen Mary II, ruling monarchs of England at the time.

King and Queen is sometimes called the Shoestring County, because its average width is only eight miles and its length is sixty-five.

TOLSTOY, SOUTH DAKOTA

A number of families who had migrated from Russia had settled in this region in the early 1900's. They tried to retain a bit of the old country by naming their new home Tolstoy, after the famous Russian writer. Count Leo Tolstoi was still living at the time.

TRIBUNE, KANSAS

This entire region was named in honor of the newspapermen who put out the famed New York *Tribune*. Tribune itself is located in Greeley County, named after Horace Greeley, the paper's famous founder. Nearby is another small town named Horace. A railroad siding was named Whitelaw, and a regional town was called Reid, both of them for the newspaper's editor, Whitelaw Reid.

Founders of Towns

NEW FREEDOM, PENNSYLVANIA

A family named Free came to this part of Pennsylvania in 1783. Their ancestry can be traced back to France, a country that the persecuted De Ferrees fled from in 1685 with thousands of other Huguenot families.

This Pennsylvania town recognized the contributions of the generations of Frees by naming the borough New Freedom. In 1873 it was made official.

It is historically interesting that a town called Freeland, just south of New Freedom below the Mason-Dixon line, was a stop-off station for the Underground Railroad before the Civil War. When escaping slaves reached here, they were in "Freeland, which was not free, but when they crossed the line into Pennsylvania a few miles north, they had reached a "new freedom."

NAPOLEON, NORTH DAKOTA

This town was named, not for Bonaparte, but for Napoleon Goodsill, a member of the company that surveyed and sold the original lots.

HUMBLE, TEXAS

Around 1889, Pleasant Smith Humble settled this region with his family, cutting timber into railroad ties, keeping store, and serving as justice of the peace. Twenty-two years and several oil gushers later, big-time oil operators incorporated a company in the area, calling it Humble Oil, the forerunner of one of the biggest petroleum producers in the world.

JOB, WEST VIRGINIA

Job Parsons, a prominent businessman, stockman, and farmer, operated the first post office and local store in this region.

MACBETH, SOUTH CAROLINA

In 1704 the Lords Proprietors of Carolina granted this tract of land (in what is now Berkeley County) to a Frenchman by the name of Phillip Trovillart. Through the years ownership changed hands thirteen times before coming to Charles MacBeth, owner of the local store and sawmill.

BIRD CITY, KANSAS

In the last half of the nineteenth century, this was cattle country. At that time, the Northwest Land Cattle Company of St. Joseph, Missouri, sent Benjamin Bird here to manage its new location. Bird became so known and respected by the influx of people that they decided to name the town in his honor.

MARS, PENNSYLVANIA

Local residents say the town was named in honor of Samuel Marshall, a man who helped establish the town's first post office in 1873.

McCAMEY, TEXAS

Before 1920, nary a soul could be seen in this area. Then, an adventurous Irish driller named McCamey brought in a big oil gusher. Soon the new town of McCamey was booming, with 10,000 people living in tents and other types of rapidly built dwellings.

RINGLING, OKLAHOMA

John Ringling, of the Ringling Brothers Circus, furnished the money for an important railroad, which was supposed to go to Cornish, Oklahoma.

However, a dispute arose with the city fathers of Cornish, which led Ringling to divert the railroad about a mile north of the original route. He then bought up land in that section of the region and established a town that bore his name.

CRAFTSBURY COMMON, VERMONT

The town's name was changed from Minden to Craftsbury in 1790 to honor Colonel Ebenezer Crafts, a leader in the move from Massachusetts to this settlement.

"Common," the second half of the name, stems from the town common, a large tract of land on top of the hill where the village was located. The settlers held this area in common, planting such crops as potatoes on it and then dividing the harvest among the families. At other times it was used as a community pasture ground.

Prominent Local People

OGLETHORPE, GEORGIA

The city of Oglethorpe was named for James Edward Oglethorpe, founder and administrator of Georgia, the last of the thirteen English colonies to be established on the American mainland. He often visited the Creek Indians who lived in this region.

General Oglethorpe began settling the colony in 1733, intending to make it a haven for imprisoned English debtors and for persecuted Protestants.

The hamlet of Oglethorpe was incorporated by the Georgia legislature on December 14, 1840. The local population at the time was 268 whites and 186 blacks. Soon the railroad came, and the town grew in leaps and bounds. There was a move to make Oglethorpe the capital of Georgia, but in the plebiscite, it was defeated by one vote.

In 1855 the city had a population of 20,000, and a downtown district that had eighty business houses, ten large cotton warehouses, eight stables, and four large hotels. In 1862 an epidemic of smallpox struck the area, taking numerous lives. Many people left, and rows of houses were burned. The present population of Oglethorpe is less than 1,500.

DEVINE, TEXAS

This Texas town was named after Thomas Jefferson Devine. In 1861 Devine became a member of the Confederate Secession Convention and was appointed to the Committee of Public Safety which took over the government of Texas. He and two other men then demanded the surrender of federal troops and supplies in that state. The Confederate government also appointed him a judge of the Western Judicial District, and used his services as a mediator to resolve a dispute they were involved in with Mexico.

After the Civil War, Devine was imprisoned and later indicted for high treason. However, he was pardoned by President Andrew Johnson in 1867, without ever going to trial.

In later years he concluded his adventurous career by becoming an associate justice of the Texas Supreme Court and a regent for the projected new state university.

LOVELAND, COLORADO

The town of Loveland was born on a sixty-four-acre wheat field donated by David Burns in 1877. It was named after W. A. H. Loveland, who was then president of the Colorado Central Railroad. Loveland was a soldier, statesman, educator, railroad builder—one of Colorado's most colorful sons.

Loveland is now known as the Sweetheart City because of the large number of valentines that are annually remailed from the local postoffice. Each year, more than 100,000 people from all over the country send their Valentine Day cards here to get the colorful Loveland stamp.

MOSES, WEST VIRGINIA

The town was named for a local general superintendent of mines, Harry M. Moses, who helped negotiate many soft-coal contracts with the late John L. Lewis, head of the coal miners and organizer of the CIO.

LAWYERSVILLE, NEW YORK

This hamlet in Schoharie County was first called The Patent, a name that had been taken from the original grant of land ceded to Goldsbrow Banyar in 1752. It contained about four thousand acres.

The name was changed to Lawyersville about 1819 by General Thomas Lawyer (a lawyer), who used his influence as a newly elected member of Congress to have a post office established here.

Interestingly enough, the town never lacked lawyers, having as many as three in its early years.

VALENTINE, NEBRASKA

This settlement began in 1878, the year the federal government moved more than five thousand Sioux Indians to the nearby Rosebud Reservation. The name Valentine was in honor of Congressman E. K. Valentine, who was elected from this district.

Each year, on February 14, Valentine Day, this whole town celebrates. As in Loveland, Colorado, an important event is the stamping of valentine cards and letters that have been sent to the post office and the local chamber of commerce.

SALAMANCA, NEW YORK

Men had come to this region in the early 1800's, but did not remain. The area first began to develop as a result of the railroad yards that Señor Salamanca, a Spanish-born banker, helped establish. He was an important stockholder in the Atlantic and Great Western Railroad.

UNCLE SAM, LOUISIANA

On the east bank of the Mississippi River, between Donaldsonville and Convent, lay an extensive plantation called Uncle Sam. It was built in the late 1830's by Pierre Auguste Fagot, a sugar planter.

GARY, WEST VIRGINIA

Gary is principally a coal-mining community engaged in supplying high-quality metallurgical Pocahontas coal to the stell mills. The region was developed by the United States Steel Corporation in the early 1900's.

The person chiefly responsible for this immense undertaking was Judge Elbert H. Gary, an early founder of U. S. Steel. The mines in Gary, West Virginia, supply coal to the giant steel-producing plants in Gary, Indiana, also named for the judge. Elbert, West Virginia, also bears his name.

When the mines first opened, people heard of jobs available and migrated to the new community. Black Americans came from North Carolina, Virginia, Tennessee, and Alabama, white Europeans sailed from Italy, Poland, Czechoslovakia, Yugoslavia, Spain, Greece, and Germany, and experienced miners of English, Welsh, Scotch, and Irish descent brought their families from the Pennsylvania coalfields.

JUNEAU, ALASKA

Juneau, the capital of Alaska, had several other names before a miners' meeting chose the present one on December 14, 1881. The Indians gave it a name that meant "flounder creek" and used the region as their summer fishing camp. The first prospectors called it Pilzburg or Fliptown. United States Navy men, stationed here in 1881 to maintain the law, called it Rockwell, the name of their commander. And the post office got into the act by naming their unit Harrisburg.

It was eventually named for Joseph Juneau, a local prospector who was born in Quebec and raised in Wisconsin. His gold fever was eventually cured when he and Richard Harris made a big strike at Gold Creek. However, Mr. Juneau's fortune soon passed through his fingers, and he wound up owning a small restaurant in an Alaskan town.

Well Known

LULING, TEXAS

This is a town named for Lu Ling, a Chinese restaurant owner who served the men who built the Galveston, Harrisburg, and San Antonio Railway.

CHARLESTON, OREGON

Like many towns in America, Charleston got its name from people identifying a place with someone who lived there. In this situation, it was a Chinese laborer named Charlie who had settled in the region.

Named for Women

JOSEPHINE COUNTY, OREGON

On January 22, 1856, three years before Oregon became a state, its territorial legislature made this its eighteenth county—the only one named after a woman. When Miss Josephine Rollins arrived here in 1851 with her father, who was seeking his fortune as a miner, she became the first white woman to settle in this part of Oregon. The miners struck paydirt in a local creek, which is still called Josephine Creek.

During the same time period English sailors, who had deserted their ship at Crescent City, found their way into this region and successfully discovered rich gold fields in the Illinois Valley. The area was known for a long time as Sailor Diggings.

MARY ESTHER, FLORIDA

A Presbyterian minister, John Newton, named this Civil War town for his two daughters, Mary and Esther. It was adjacent to Camp Walton, a Confederate military installation.

PEACE DALE, RHODE ISLAND

In 1793, Rowland Hazard named this town for his bride, Mary Peace.

GYPSY, WEST VIRGINIA

In 1900 the governor of the state was given the privilege of naming this town in Harrison County, because of the financial interest he had in its coal mine. He named it after his niece Gypsy.

DELIA, KANSAS

Delia Cunningham bought this tract of land from Ann Nolan on April 10, 1873, for $612. Several years later she sold it to her own son, David, for twice that amount. At the turn of the century he got a handsome return on his investment when he sold the northern part of his land—bisected by railroad tracts—to the Delia Town Site Company. He did this with the understanding that he would be allowed to use the name "Delia" when he incorporated his section. However, to his consternation, businessmen from the southern tract incorporated their site with his mother's name. Quite angry, David then had his land, on the north side, incorporated as the city of David, naming it after his father and, in effect, creating "mom and pop" towns.

As time went on, the entire area became known as Delia, officially acquiring that name in 1971, a century after Delia Cunningham bought the land.

ALICE, TEXAS

Named after the daughter of one of the founders of the famous King Ranch.

SARITA, TEXAS

Named for Sarita Kennedy, granddaughter of Mifflin Kennedy, an associate of Richard King, founder of the King Ranch.

DONNA, TEXAS

Named for the daughter of the town site's promoter and first postmaster.

MERCEDES, TEXAS

Named for Mercedes Díaz, wife of Porfirio Díaz, Mexican President. It was originally settled in the late 1770's by Mexican ranchers who held a Spanish grant.

INSPIRED NAMES

Inspired by the Bible

Religion has played a significant role in the exploration and settlement of many areas in America. The Spanish conquistadors and French missionaries named their discoveries after saints, centuries before other religious movements sought havens in the New World. The power of faith has caused people to travel over rolling seas and through torrid deserts to settle new lands. The names of their communities were reflections of their devout determination.

MACEDONIA, OHIO

The first settlers in this area wanted a clergyman but were too poor to hire one. In their need they called upon the seminary in nearby Hudson, Ohio, to send someone to their settlement to conduct services. The student ministers looked upon these requests as a "Macedonian call," which had been mentioned in Acts 16:9. Paul had seen, in a vision, "a man of Macedonia" asking him to "come over into Macedonia and help us." This inspired the community to give this name to their town.

BABYLON, NEW YORK

Around 1800 the inhabitants of this area, Methodist and Presbyterians, frowned upon the drinking that others in the community engaged in. They thus decided to name their town New Babylon in an attempt to distinguish it from the biblical Babylon that was steeped in luxury and wickedness.

DAMASCUS, MARYLAND

The deeply religious settlers here probably took this name from the Bible, as did other communities in the nearby towns of Mount Tabor, Mount Lebanon, Mount Radnor, Mount Zion, Bethel, and Bethesda.

Settled by Religious Groups

ZION, ILLINOIS

John Alexander Dowie, a faith-healing minister, founded this city in 1901. Dowie, an Australian, started his religious movement, the Christian Catholic Church, in Chicago. Having achieved great success there, he bought six thousand acres on the shores of Lake Michigan to develop a city that he hoped would be Utopia on earth. In a few years the population of the city grew to ten thousand. It had its own school system, and the movement's parishioners worked in the town's industries, giving their earnings to the church.

This planned community, originally called the City of Zion, also has biblical names for its north–south streets.

BETHLEHEM, PENNSYLVANIA

The Moravians, a religious sect from Germany, had settled in this part of Pennsylvania to live and practice their Christian beliefs. On Christmas Eve, 1741, their patron, Count Zinzendorf, led his congregation into the stable that adjoined the main house, singing the German hymn, "*Nicht Jerusalem, sondern Bethlehem, aus dir kommet was mir frommet. . . .*" ("Not Jerusalem but Bethlehem, out of thee cometh what profiteth me.") Thereafter, the name Bethlehem, which was previously the name for the big house, was now taken by the whole community.

NEW HAVEN, CONNECTICUT

In the 1630's a number of Puritans from England established a settlement called Quinnipiac. The name was soon changed to New Haven Colony, a place they hoped would be a haven for their families.

TABERNACLE, NEW JERSEY

At the turn of the century white residents shared this site, one of the first reservations in the United States, with the Lenni Lenape (Delaware) tribe.

The settlers had erected a building here known to all in the Shamong Township as the Tabernacle. They used it to hold services and store their winter provisions. Food was given to the Indians, who, in turn, were asked to attend these Sunday services. Later, the town officially took the name of this central building.

SHAKER HEIGHTS, OHIO

The Shakers are a religious commune in which men and women do not marry or have children. Founded in England by Mother Ann Lee as an offshoot of Quakerism, the sect was brought to America in 1774 and established in New York and New Hampshire. Ralph Russell led a group to Ohio in 1822, where they settled near Cleveland. This Shaker Heights colony disbanded in 1889, and the land was sold to a commercial firm and developed as a residential community.

A hard-working people, Shakers consider all individuals equal, regardless of race, sex, color, or position in society. Shaker women have long had equal rights and leadership positions with men, and the society has always welcomed Indians and blacks as equal members. Unfortunately, the society has decided to take in no new members, and when the last of the remaining elders and sisters dies, the sect will be extinct.

Inspired by Saints

SAN DIEGO, CALIFORNIA

In 1542, fifty years after Columbus came to the New World, the conquistador Juan Rodriguez Cabrillo claimed this West Coast area for Spain. In November 1602, Sebastian Vizcaino, another Spanish explorer, named the region. He noted in his ship's journal the momentous event:

The next day, Sunday, the 10th of the month, we arrived at a port which must be the best to be found in all the South Seas. . . . On the

12th of the said month, which was the day of the glorious San Diego, the general, admiral, religious, captains, ensigns, and almost all the men went ashore. A hut was built and mass was said in celebration of the feast of Señor San Diego.

Diego is the Spanish for James, one of the twelve Apostles, who is credited with being the person who first preached Christianity in Spain.

ST. PAUL, MINNESOTA

Several years before St. Paul got its present name, it was known as Pig's Eye for a well-known sailor and tavern owner named Pierre "Pig's Eye" Parrant.

The city was renamed in 1841 by Father Lucien Galtier, the first Catholic priest to establish a mission here. He wrote about the naming:

In the month of October, logs were prepared and a church erected, so poor that it would well remind one of the stable at Bethlehem. It was destined, however, to be the nucleus of a great city. On the first day of November, I blessed the new basilica, and dedicated it to Saint Paul, the apostle of nations.

PANNA MARIA, TEXAS

This community, established in 1854, may be the oldest Polish settlement in America. The Polish Catholic immigrants fulfilled their vow to name their new town *Panna Maria* ("Miss Mary"), meaning the Virgin Mary.

SAN FRANCISCO, CALIFORNIA

In 1595 a name honoring Saint Francis of Assisi was given to this region on the Pacific coast. In 1769 the explorer Gaspar de Portola discovered the great bay and applied the name specifically to it.

The city itself was named officially on March 10, 1847, by General Stephen W. Kearny, American military governor.

ST. LOUIS, MISSOURI

In 1764 this great city was founded by a Frenchman, Pierre Laclède, and his fourteen-year-old stepson, Auguste Chouteau.

Their venture had begun a year earlier, when they led a group of frontiersmen up the Mississippi River from the French town of New Orleans. They then explored the region, determined to find a good place for a fur-trading post. Coming upon an ideal area, Laclede turned to Auguste and said: "Here are all the advantages one could desire to found a settlement which might become considerable hereafter. . . . As soon as navigation opens, you will return here and will cause to form a settlement after a plan that I shall give you." When his plan became a reality, he named the new settlement after Louis IX, a thirteenth-century king of France, who was canonized for his piety and justice.

Inspired by Imagination

In a country as broad and diverse as the United States, there are many types of people, who are motivated in many different ways. Some want their towns to have foreign names, others want them named after famous persons. Then there are those dreamy-eyed individuals who get inspired by a bolt from the blue.

INSPIRATION, ARIZONA

It is said that a Scottish prospector was led to a rich mining claim by a vision or inspiration, and thus gave this name to his find.

MONTEZUMA, COLORADO

This mining town was named in 1865 for the last Aztec ruler of Mexico, who had fabulous amounts of gold. The first miners in the area thought it to be an appropriate name because they expected the town to become as rich as the emperor was.

MATADOR, TEXAS

Back in 1879 several men pooled their money and established what was to become one of the biggest ranches in west Texas. A partner in the venture, W. Lomax, persuaded the others to name the ranch Matador. He was an avid reader of Spanish literature and greatly admired the valiant bullfighters.

NEW ERA, MICHIGAN

The owner of the local sawmill wanted to call the community New Erie, after his former home in Erie, Pennsylvania, but other citizens preferred a different name. They compromised, feeling that they could name the town for the "new era" they were living in. It surely was! During that year, 1873, the first elevator was installed in an office building, patents were granted for the typewriter, and the telephone was on its way.

ECLECTIC, ALABAMA

After the Civil War, a young physician, Dr. M. L. Fielder, returned home and began to develop a new town. He had been educated in a northern school, which offered a course of study in "eclectic" medicine. "Eclectic" means something composed of elements from various sources.

This seems to have been Dr. Fielder's intention for his new town, because he offered to donate one acre to any person, white or black, who would build a home in Eclectic.

STAR, NORTH CAROLINA

The story goes that Angus Leach was sitting one night, looking at the stars, when he saw one that was shining with special brightness. This inspired him to say, "That's it—I'll name the town Star and long may it shine."

EXCEL, ALABAMA

M. D. Harrison, original homesteader of the town, gave its post office the name "Excel" in 1884. He thought the region would excel because of the agricultural potential of the excellent surrounding farmlands.

OASIS, UTAH

When John Styler came to this area in Utah, there was nothing but greasewood, rabbit brush, and other desolation. He immediately began to plant cottonwood trees along irrigation ditches, creating his dream—an oasis in the desert.

LITTLE AMERICA, WYOMING

Back in the 1930's, a man named Covey came upon this desert area and named the site Little America in honor of Admiral Byrd's station in Antarctica. Seeing his discovery as desolate as the polar regions, Covey wanted to build a stop-off place for weary travelers.

The Little America post office still gets letters from members of the Antarctic expedition, who request the town's postmark.

NAMES FROM LOCAL TOPOGRAPHY

The natural beauty of our three million square miles has appealed to many town namers. So have the distinctive quirks of topography that give a locality a look all its own.

Rock Formations

DEVIL'S SLIDE, UTAH

The town was named for a huge limestone rock formation, which looks like a deep, carved-out sliding pond. The early settlers believed the devil slid down it.

ROUND BUTTE, MONTANA

In this Rocky Mountain valley near Flathead Lake, a community developed around a small, steep mountain, or butte, from which it got its name.

NATURAL BRIDGE, VIRGINIA

This huge limestone bridge is 215 feet high and 90 feet long, and has a 49-foot arch. Several cars could easily ride side by side across its width. It was carved over a period of millions of years by the eroding forces of a creek that ran into the James River.

In 1778 Thomas Jefferson personally acquired the Natural Bridge and 157 surrounding acres for a mere twenty shillings. Thereafter, Jefferson came here frequently to view and chart his holdings. Another Founding Father, George Washington, had previously surveyed the site for Lord Fairfax, leaving his initials at the base of the bridge.

MEXICAN HAT, UTAH

Near this town in southeastern Utah, there is a natural rock formation on top of a little mountain, which looks like a head wearing a large Mexican sombrero.

BIG STONE CITY, SOUTH DAKOTA

When the Dakota Sioux Indians saw huge boulders on the shore of a local lake forty miles long, they called the region the place of the Big Stones.

Today these large granite rocks constitute part of the famous Mahogany Granite Quarries, the largest source of colored granite in the world.

Water Formations

ALLIGATOR, MISSISSIPPI

This town was named after a nearby lake, which is shaped like an alligator. The name was originally Alligator Lake, but in the early 1930's it was changed to plain Alligator.

ROCKSPRINGS, TEXAS

In the late 1800's Indians and wagon-train pioneers found springs in this area. This excellent source of fresh water was located at the highest level of a rugged plateau known locally as the Hill Country.

RED BOILING SPRINGS, TENNESSEE

In 1840 Shepherd Kirby came with his family to this part of Tennessee to begin a better life.

While he was hewing logs for his new house, he came upon a spring, which he then used to bathe his chronically infected eyes. The mineral waters in the spring not only soothed the ailment, but after several treatments completely cured it. Thereafter, the news of the magical powers of the water spread rapidly, bringing people with various sorts of disorders from all parts of the territory.

Scientifically, the many springs and wells of this area become mineralized when ground water comes in contact with the local Chattanooga shale formation. The bubbling (or "boiling") springs get their red color and rotten-egg odor from pyrite, an iron sulfide mineral.

MINERAL WELLS, TEXAS

The medicinal properties of the water in this region made it nationally famous, drawing thousands of health seekers. It was believed that one of the wells, called Crazy Well, could cure mental illness.

HONOLULU, HAWAII

Honolulu, meaning "sheltered harbor," was a key shipping point in the Pacific. Seamen, adventurers, merchants, and missionaries from all parts of the world came to this Hawaiian port. The Polynesian people settled in Hawaii well before A.D. 1000.

In 1804 Hawaiian King Kamehameha, after uniting all the islands in a major battle in Nuuanu Valley, moved his court from the big island of Hawaii to the city of Honolulu on Oahu.

ZIGZAG, OREGON

The Zigzag River was so named because of its winding course down the lower slopes of Mount Hood. The same name was later given to a small village, a glacier, a mountain, and a canyon in the region.

SACRED HEART, MINNESOTA

In the late 1850's a missionary group, traveling down the Minnesota River, turned up a tributary creek, where they discovered an unusual sand formation. The current had created a sandbar in the shape of a heart. Their leader, a Jesuit priest, thereupon named the creek Sacred Heart (for the Sacred Heart of Jesus, a Roman Catholic devotion), placing a wooden cross there to mark the spot.

A post office was later established in the region and named Sacred Heart, and eventually a village in the township took the same name.

SIOUX FALLS, SOUTH DAKOTA

The city got its name from natural waterfalls that empty into the Big Sioux River. The Sioux Indians called the river *Wakpa-Ipaktan,* which means "winding," because it forms a huge "S" as it meanders downstream to join the Missouri River.

BRIDAL VEIL, OREGON

One hundred years ago, a woman passenger on a Columbia River steamboat noticed very pretty waterfalls on the Oregon side of that body of water. The lovely sight prompted her to remark: "That looks like a bride's veil." The name stuck and in later years, it became the official designation of the local depot, post office, and town.

Local Flora and Fauna

LOOKINGGLASS, OREGON

Pioneers who went through this valley during the spring months in the mid-nineteenth century were pleased to see the vast fields of flowering blue camas. The flowers seemed to reflect the blue of the sky, creating a looking-glass effect.

During an earlier period, Lookingglass Valley was occasionally called Mirror Vale.

LIVELY, VIRGINIA

The town of Lively, established on March 2, 1833, was a shortening of "Lively Oak," an estate that was so named for the many tall, stately oak trees that graced the property.

LEBANON, NEW HAMPSHIRE

This is another example of a place name taken from an earlier American town—in this instance, Lebanon, Connecticut, which, it is said, had a swamp of cedar trees that reminded its settlers of the cedars of Lebanon in Asia Minor.

The New Hampshire town is a member of a famous triad of communities whose names comprise a popular local joke: Orange, Lebanon, and Lyme.

TUPELO, MISSISSIPPI

This town, named for native tupelo gum trees, had its beginning in the mid-nineteenth century with one store, two saloons, and a temporary railroad station.

Tupelo is a Creek Indian word meaning "swamp tree." These tall trees usually grow in swampland.

PAW PAW, MICHIGAN

This area of Michigan was explored by Jesuit missionaries in the seventeenth century. On one of their maps they inscribed the name "Paw Paw" for the local river that flowed through a large glacial valley. The name was probably taken from the papaw (*Asimina triloba*), a shrub or small tree (related to the tropical custard-apple family), which grows abundantly along the river's bottom.

EDEN, VERMONT

It is said that early settlers, who found a great variety of wildflowers and plants growing here in a peat bog, thought it resembled the Garden of Eden.

ORANGE, TEXAS

Boatmen who navigated the Sabine River noticed orange groves on the shore, and thereafter referred to this area as Orange. The town was established in 1836, the year Texas won its independence from Mexico.

FALFURRIAS, TEXAS

The town was named in 1883 for a local wildflower, the falfurrias.

BLACK EAGLE, MONTANA

The explorers Lewis and Clark, in their 1805 expedition, observed a pair of black eagles nesting on a small island directly below beautiful cascading waterfalls. They referred to it in their diary as Black Eagle Falls.

MOSQUERO, NEW MEXICO

Mosquero is Spanish for "swarm of flies," a fitting description for the buffalo herds and their accompanying swarms of flies that once roamed this area.

BLACKBIRD, DELAWARE

According to Clifford Pryor, an early resident of the area, Blackbird was named by the early settlers for the large flocks of blackbirds that settled in the area, particularly during the fall migration season.

Sometimes they were, and still are, so numerous that it often takes an hour for a flock to pass overhead. I recall that once when we were hauling corn they were so thick around us that I fired a muzzle-loading gun, loaded with fine shot, into a flock and picked up a bushel basket full of dead birds. We cut out the breasts of about "four and twenty" of them and persuaded Mother to make them in a pie. The pie was huge, and looked grand, but the birds did not come out to sing as they did in the old English rhyme. They were not such a dainty dish either.

MARIPOSA, CALIFORNIA

Mariposa is the Spanish word for "butterfly." In 1806, when Spanish explorers passed through this area, the bushes along the creek were covered with *mariposas*.

HORSE HEAVEN, OREGON

This place in Jefferson County, once the home of numerous horses, is no longer populated by people or their mounts. Ada McKee, an eighty-year-old resident of the county, noted how the region had changed:

I haven't seen a draft horse here in years except at state fairs or horse shows in Portland. [Nowadays] one might sit on our main street a year and never see a horse. How different from my early years when I rode my pony to bring in the milk cows and to school, and delivered the cream to the creamery in a top buggy. That was pleasure combined with work.

Border Towns

TEXHOMA, OKLAHOMA

This town, located in the Oklahoma panhandle but squarely on the Texas border, was the last part of the state to be settled. A combination of the two state names was a natural for it.

Texhoma has residents in both Oklahoma and Texas, with the majority of businesses in the former. Each state also has its own elementary school, but there is only one high school—in Oklahoma.

TEXARKANA, TEXAS

In the 1870's this was the point on the Texas–Arkansas border where two great railroads merged, the Cairo and Fulton, and the Texas and Pacific. At the time of the town's naming, it was mistakenly believed that Louisiana was only a few miles south, thus the name, Tex-Ark-*Ana*. Actually Louisiana lies nearly 150 miles away.

CALEXICO, CALIFORNIA

This town in Imperial County lies directly across the border from the more famous Mexicali, Mexico.

High Places

EMINENCE, KENTUCKY

In the mid 1800's this town was the highest point of elevation on the Louisville and Nashville Railroad.

ALTO, TEXAS

This was the highest point between the Angelina and Neches Rivers, and was thus given the Spanish name *Alto*—"high." It was originally a stop on the Old San Antonio Road.

CLIMAX, COLORADO

During the second half of the nineteenth century, this central region of Colorado was known for its gold and silver mines. Prospectors who traveled here by railroad crossed from east to west Colorado over a mountaintop called Fremont Pass. The pass was 11,318 feet above sea level, which was the high point or "climax" of the railroad. This name was later adopted by the town that developed it.

Unique Locations

MESOPOTAMIA, OHIO

In 1819 this five-square-mile area was named Mesopotamia because of its geographical similarities to the land in the Middle East (now called Iraq). The ancient Mesopotamia was located between the Tigris and Euphrates rivers, and the new city is situated between the Grand and Cuyahoga rivers. The word *mesopotamia* is the Greek for "between rivers."

CUBA, ILLINOIS

Cuba was, in all likelihood, named for the island of the same name, the largest in the West Indies. In its early years this region was like an island, surrounded by ponds on every side. In addition, the Illinois town of Havana was only twenty miles away.

STAR CITY, ARKANSAS

In the younger days of this town, Dr. John S. Simmons, a founding father, noticed that the settlement was located in the middle of a group of hills which looked like the points of a star. He then persuaded the townspeople to change its name to Star City.

BUFFALO GAP, TEXAS

Buffalo, for hundreds of years, traveled through this natural pass in the Callahan Divide. It was also later used by cattlemen to drive their herds to the Dodge City market.

Large Geographical Regions

DEATH VALLEY, CALIFORNIA

From 1848 to 1850 emigrants who crossed the country on their way to the Sierra Nevada gold fields passed through this unbearably hot and grueling valley. Later, others came back to the valley to mine for gold and other minerals, such as borax.

The region was given the name Death Valley as a result of the suffering endured by these pioneering men and women.

SUPERIOR, WISCONSIN

This city is located at the tip of Lake Superior, the largest body of fresh water in the world.

PANHANDLE, TEXAS

This wheat, cattle, and oil town was so named because of its geographical location in the heart of the Texas panhandle. A "panhandle," of course, is a narrow strip of land that juts out from the main bulk of a state, like the handle of a pan. Oklahoma and Florida also have panhandles.

NAMES FROM
UNIQUE SITUATIONS

Names from a Specialty of the Area

A basic, and perhaps the most logical, way to name a community is to describe the type of activity that takes place within it. Examples of this range from New Mexico's Pie Town to Idaho's Atomic City.

PIE TOWN, NEW MEXICO

In 1919 a soldier who was mustered out of the army moved to the West to make his fortune. He soon opened a gasoline station in this section of New Mexico, but business was a little slow, so he started frying little fruit pies to add to his income. A local couple saw the potential profit in pies and began selling baked ones in their little grocery store. When the time came for a post office and town name, a cowboy, who had been buying groceries and pies, suggested Pie Town. All agreed.

EXCHANGE, WEST VIRGINIA

This region had been a natural center for a farming community since the days of the earliest settlers. In the late 1800's the local general store changed ownership so often that the neighborhood was named Exchange.

HELPER, UTAH

This little town is located in the mountains about twenty miles from Soldier Summit, a high point in the area. Long ago, when railroad and freight trains had difficulty making the climb to the Summit, engines from this town would help by pushing them up the hill. They thus decided to name their community Helper.

REFUGIO, TEXAS

Throughout the southwest, Spanish friars built missions where people could come for help. The last such mission in Texas, *Nuestra Señora del Refugio*, "Our Lady of Refuge," was located in this area.

LIBRARY, PENNSYLVANIA

In 1833 John Moore and his friends decided to give their town a solid educational foundation by establishing a library. They were soon able to buy two thousand books from money that they had collected from community residents. The new library, which was kept in Moore's home, was supported by individual annual dues of $1.50. The last librarian was Samuel Wilson, the local blacksmith, who stored the old library in his stable.

HEREFORD, TEXAS

This city got its name from the internationally famous Hereford breed of cattle that were moved here in 1902. The cattle had been named after the English city of Hereford, a name meaning "army crossing." The city got this name in A.D. 700 when the West Saxons crossed the River Wye at this site and established a settlement on the edge of Wales.

SPEEDWAY, INDIANA

In 1907 a group of men bought land here to build a racetrack in order to test the "horseless carriages." Two years later they expanded it to conduct sprint car races on a dirt surface. This was later paved with 3 million bricks, and, in time, repaved with asphalt to become the famous Indianapolis 500 Mile Racetrack. Each May more than 250,000 fans converge on this city to watch this event, one of the most famous of all car races.

Races were not held in the war years 1917–1918 and 1942–1945. The track was used as a military airfield during the earlier period, after America's entry into World War I.

ELECTRIC CITY, WASHINGTON

The town was named in honor of the newly constructed Grand Coulee Dam, which supplies electricity to all of the Pacific Northwest.

COMBINED LOCKS, WISCONSIN

This village is located on the Fox River, between Lake Winnebago and the city of Green Bay. There is a substantial change in elevation between these two points, which has made it necessary to have dams equipped with locks up and down the river. The locks are used to raise or lower the boats that pass through. Most of the river's locks are twenty feet high, but the elevation adjacent to this village drops twice as much as the others—forty feet. This has made it necessary to have two adjoining locks, or "combined locks," at this section of the dam—an unusual situation.

Pleasure boats have now replaced coal and pulp-wood barges along the Fox River, one of the largest among the rivers in the world that flow away from the equator.

EXPERIMENT, GEORGIA

In 1889 the University of Georgia's College of Agriculture established an experimental station in this area.

ATOMIC CITY, IDAHO

The space age came to this small town in 1950, when the United States Atomic Energy Commission built the National Reactor Testing Station near here. When the town got a post office, they decided to change their name from Midway to Atomic City.

Spur-of-the-Moment Names

Strange as it may seem, many American towns got their names from a casual remark someone has made.

Towns usually began with a small number of families, followed by other settlers, then a post office. If something unusual was said or done in one of these small communities, it was soon known throughout the entire region. Sometimes, the anecdote stuck and became the town's name.

BLESSING, TEXAS

When the railroad people were pushing southward at the turn of the century, they allowed landowners who offered them the right of way the privilege of naming the post office that would be constructed on their property. One of these big pieces of land was owned by a J. E. Pierce, whom the railroad officials visited to discuss a post-office name. He told them he picked the name "Thank God" because that was the way he felt about having a railroad right on his ranch. The railroad men had visions of train conductors walking through the car, calling out: "Thank God, Thank God, all off for Thank God."

Another official was sent to get a different name from Pierce. Diplomatically he humored the rancher by talking of the blessing of having a railroad on his property. Pierce soon took the word "blessing" as his own idea, and suggested that the stop be called Blessing.

MOROCCO, INDIANA

In 1851, as several workmen were cutting timber for the western boundary of their new town, a stranger on horseback dismounted and approached them, asking for directions. He was unusual in that he wore a pair of high boots which were topped with shining red morocco leather. The workmen were so impressed with this sight that they prevailed upon the settlers to name the town Morocco. They even called the avenue they were working on Walker Street, because of the stranger's rapid strides.

SOCIAL CIRCLE, GEORGIA

Some say that on a Saturday night long ago, when a group of townsmen were sitting around a bonfire, a stranger walked up and was immediately invited to join the conversation. Pleasantly surprised at such friendliness, he commented: "This is surely a social circle."

VALUE, MISSISSIPPI

The townspeople in this area, so the story goes, were pondering a name for a post office that had been promised to them. One day a black man came into the local general store, speaking with what some of them thought was an affected Chicago accent. Looking at the merchandise, he kept asking the storeowner what the "value" of certain items were, instead of just how much they cost. The incident so amused the local people that they gave the name to their town.

SEARCHLIGHT, NEVADA

This town was founded in 1898 after the discovery of the local Duplex Mine. The story goes that someone remarked that there was gold there, but it took a searchlight to find it.

DEFIANCE, OHIO

In 1794 America was once again very close to war with England, because the British were helping the Indian tribes in the Northwest Territory prevent the new republic from taking control of that region. A concerned President Washington sent General Anthony Wayne to the area with orders to take back the territory. Wayne, with more than four thousand men, many of them Kentucky sharpshooters, carefully moved down the Maumee River, building forts as he went. At one of these forts he uttered: "I defy the English, the Indians, and all the Devils in Hell to take it." A general, standing nearby, said: "Then call it Fort Defiance." And so it became known.

On August 20, 1794, Wayne met and defeated the Indians in the famous Battle of Fallen Timbers, which effectively ended Great Britain's hopes of keeping control of the territory.

Defiance is also noteworthy for other interesting occurrences. It was the scene, in 1793, of the largest Indian powwow ever held in North America—the council of all the Indian tribes in the area. Attending were tribal chiefs from the Miamis, Shawnees, Wyandots, Senecas, Ottawas, Delawares, Kickapoos, Potawatomis, Ojibway, and Mohawks.

A famous Defiance resident was John Chapman, known throughout America as Johnny Appleseed. He came here in 1811, at the age of thirty-seven, and remained for seventeen years while growing his pioneer apple orchards.

ONG'S HAT, NEW JERSEY

One of several name legends for this little hamlet tells us that Jacob Ong, a dancer and a ladies' man, always used to wear his shiny hat to the

Saturday night dances at the local taverns. On one such occasion Mr. Ong did not pay sufficient attention to a certain lady friend, who grew annoyed, angrily grabbed his hat, threw it to the floor, and proceeded to stamp it out of shape.

RESCUE, VIRGINIA

The area's first postmaster, William T. Carter, was given the right to name the post office. He chose the name Rescue because of the feeling he used to get when his district's mail was delivered. It was brought from a distant post office by a man riding a mule. Carter would always comment at the sight of the delivery that "the mail was rescued from the mule's back."

COMFORT, TEXAS

In 1854, German settlers, exhausted from their journey from New Braunfels, Texas, saw a beautiful site with rolling hills and pure water. They named it Camp Comfort.

In present-day Comfort, the whole town celebrates each Fourth of July with a community barbecue and traditional German band music and dancing.

FAIRDEALING, MISSOURI

Many years ago, according to town legend, while a traveler was passing through this area, his horse went lame. A local horse trader, seeing the fellow's predicament, made him a fair offer for a good horse. The stranger was very happy. He said he would pass the word that there was fair dealing in this part of Missouri. The name stuck.

MIDNIGHT, MISSISSIPPI

According to a local tale, this small village in Humphreys County got its name as the result of a poker game. In the early years, hardworking pioneers used to get together every so often for long poker games, which might last for several days and nights. During one of these marathon sessions, one player, having lost all his money, bet his land and lost that also. The winner raked in the pot, glanced at his watch, and remarked: "Well, boys, it's midnight, and that's just what I'm going to call my new land."

ECHO, MINNESOTA

Echo township was named in 1878, and according to the village clerk, this is the story of how it got its name:

When it was time to name their community, the town board met and decided on "Rose." But this was not acceptable, for they were informed, after the state records were checked, that there was a Rose Township in Minnesota, and state law did not allow two townships to have the same name. They then chose "Empire," but this too came back with word that there was then another township with that name in the state. Finally, one of the annoyed board members said, half jokingly: "Since all the names came back, maybe we should call it 'Echo.' " And so they did.

EIGHTY EIGHT, KENTUCKY

This small rural town is located 8.8 miles east of Glasgow, which is the county seat of Barren County.

In the early years of its development, the townspeople gathered to decide on a permanent name. Mr. Dabnie Nunnally, the postmaster, said: "Let's call it Eighty Eight. I don't write very well, and I'll just use the figure 88."

An astonishing coincidence occurred here during the presidential election of 1948. When the officials counted the ballots for the town, there were 88 votes for Thomas Dewey and 88 votes for Harry S Truman.

WHY, ARIZONA

Far down in the southwestern corner of Arizona, just twenty-seven miles north of the Mexican border, a gathering of trailer court and campground people decided on the name "Why." Why? According to one resident: "Everybody wanted to know why anyone would live out in a spot like this, so we thought that would be a good name."

BERLIN, NEW JERSEY

For more than a hundred years this town was known as Long-a-Coming. How did it get this name? Local historians say that a crew of sailors shipwrecked off the New Jersey shore worked their way through dense forests seeking the cool water of a stream that the Indians told them about. They were exhausted and about to give up hope when one of them spotted the crystal-clear stream. He shouted as he threw himself into it: "Here you are, though long-a-coming." They then found their way to Philadelphia, where they described the beautiful area which became known as Long-a-Coming. It was changed to Berlin in 1867.

BUZZARDS BAY, MASSACHUSETTS

According to local legend, when English Captain Thomas Derman landed at a place called Frenchman's Creek more than three centuries ago, he saw large birds swooping and flying about. Mistaking them for buzzards, he called the region Buzzards Bay.

BAD AXE, MICHIGAN

While Captain Rudolph Papst was surveying this section of Michigan in 1861, he found, in the Indian camp he was staying at, what he considered to be an "awfully bad axe." In the minutes of his survey he named the place Bad Axe Camp.

BROKEN BOW, NEBRASKA

As often happened in the early days of the postal service, it was difficult to think of a post office name that no other community in the state used. This was the dilemma of pioneer postmaster Wilson Hewitt in 1877. His problem was resolved when his two sons, who had been playing in nearby fields, brought home a broken Indian buffalo bow. Hewitt then successfully suggested the name Broken Bow to the authorities in Washington.

CHRISTMAS, ARIZONA

In 1902 an Act of Congress officially opened for land claims what had previously been the San Carlos Apache Indian Reservation. One fellow, upon hearing the news, immediately rushed there to stake his claims on December 25, Christmas Day. He then rapidly rode on horseback to file them the next day at the government office.

SWEET HOME, OREGON

A hundred years ago, William Clark and Samuel Powell decided to live in this beautiful valley, which is tucked away in the foothills of the

Cascade Mountains. It had sparkling streams of water, fed by snow and springs from the nearby mountains.

In order to comply with the homestead laws, Clark and Powell built a double cabin on the section line, Clark sleeping on one end of the cabin and Powell sleeping on the other end. Their dining table was set in the middle of the cabin, with each man eating on his respective side.

Being quite satisfied with the promise of the region, Clark would often refer to it as his "home, sweet home," thus giving the valley and later the town their names.

RISING STAR, TEXAS

In the early 1880's, the people living here wanted to name their town Star, but a nearby community had already chosen that name. The townsfolk then called a big meeting, which lasted throughout the night until the early morning hours, without having reached agreement on a new name. However, as they left the little log schoolhouse, they saw Venus shining brightly in the eastern sky. This impelled one of them to suggest, and the others to agree, that their town be called Rising Star.

Factors other than the topography of an area, or the local Indian names, also determined a community's name. Settlers sometimes gave their home-sites names for odd happenings that took place in the vicinity. These might involve social interaction, a local occurrence, a historical event.

Names from Social Situations

FRIENDSHIP, NEW YORK

In the early 1800's, the name of this village was Fighting Corners, so called because the people in the hills and the people in the valley were always at odds with each other. Their constant feuds often ended in physical fights. Both the fighting and the town's name scared many prospective residents away. This is why, in 1815, a townsperson suggested that the name be changed to Friendship, in the hope that the new name would bring peace and people to the settlement.

TEMPERANCE, MICHIGAN

When Mr. and Mrs. Lewis Ansted sold lots from their farm, they made certain that all the deeds carried the proviso that no liquor was to be sold on the land for ninety-nine years, or it would revert to the original owners or their heirs.

This rule of social behavior concerning abstinence from drinking became the name of the local post office and town—Temperance.

DEAL ISLAND, MARYLAND

This section of Maryland, settled in 1661, was originally called Devils Island. The name was changed, probably because of church influence, which, understandably, looked unkindly on the idea of having a parish on Devils Island.

PENN YAN, NEW YORK

About 1810 a visitor to this little town could see two gristmills, a sawmill, half a dozen stores, and scattered dwelling houses. The town soon developed, and the time had come for the inhabitants—Pennsylvanians and New Englanders (Yankees), who were about equally divided in number—to choose a name. A compromise was suggested by a local man named Benjamin Barton, who wanted to call the town Penn Yank. The name was accepted, and the town eventually lost its final *k*.

Names from Local Occurrences

SOLDIER, IOWA

According to local legend, when a group of trappers came up a main river here, one of them, a former soldier, grew quite ill and died. His companions thereupon buried him on the banks of the stream and named it Soldier's River in his honor.

When Lewis and Clark explored the Missouri River in 1803, they recorded in their journal that a certain number of leagues above the place where they counciled with an Indian tribe, a beautiful stream called Soldier's River entered the Missouri.

HORSEHEADS, NEW YORK

During the Revolutionary War, General John Sullivan's troops, marching through this area, killed a number of their horses for food. The subsequent discovery here of horses' heads and skeletons caused the site to be known as Horseheads.

WINDFALL, INDIANA

People began migrating to this part of America in the 1840's. The area's first settlement was located on a creek called Wildcat, situated in the middle of heavy timber land. One day there was a terrible storm, probably a tornado, that blew down hundreds of trees. Hence, the town's name— Windfall.

EMIGRANT, MONTANA

In the days of American frontier development, numerous wagons with emigrating families crossed the Yellowstone River in a ravine near here that became known as Emigrant Gulch.

SOCIETY HILL, SOUTH CAROLINA

This town, settled in 1736, had a small wooden library building on its highest point called the Library Society on the Hill by local residents. Periodic floods and a mosquito problem forced the town to move to the higher ground near the library building. The community thereafter became known as Society Hill.

ELMIRA, NEW YORK

The village was officially named Elmira in the early 1800's for Miss Elmira Teall, a local innkeeper's daughter. It is said that the area became known by its name as a result of her mother's constant searching call— "Elmira! Elmira!"—for her little girl.

Elmira, New York, is the seat of Chemung County, an Algonkian name meaning "place of the horn." This refers to the finding of what were probably the tusks of an extinct mammoth by Indians who were preparing fields for planting corn.

WATERPROOF, LOUISIANA

This little town, about twenty miles north of Natchez, and located on the Mississippi levee, has been moved several times as a result of flooding from Old Man River.

One spring in the early 1800's floods forced a local resident, Abner Smally, to scurry to the highest point of land in the area, just barely avoiding the rising waters. As Abner sat quietly on his high, dry mound, a passing steamboat captain yelled to him: "Well, sir, I see you are waterproof." Abner liked the description and used it to denote his new home.

The residents of Waterproof still periodically move their town, as their houses and stores become part of the Mississippi River.

PASS CHRISTIAN, MISSISSIPPI

A sailor, Christian L'Adnier, discovered the inner pass leading ashore from the Gulf of Mexico to the Mississippi River. The small community that developed on the mainland near this point became known as Pass Christian.

Names from Historical Events

INDEPENDENCE, MISSOURI

The city was named as a result of patriotic feeling following celebration of the fiftieth anniversary of the Declaration of Independence in 1826.

FORTY FORT, PENNSYLVANIA

In 1769 Connecticut sent forty men to settle this fertile valley, a beautiful area that was claimed by both Pennsylvania and Connecticut. The men from Connecticut were instructed to hold the land against all comers.

During the following summer these forty pioneering settlers built a fort, establishing through blood and sweat a new American frontier. They, and others who came, had to fight Indians, the British, and Pennsylvanians to keep their land.

Forty Fort was the site of the Wyoming Valley Massacre, July 3, 1778, in which a garrison of old men and boys sallied forth to battle a raiding party of Indians and Tories and was ambushed and nearly wiped out.

COUNCIL BLUFFS, IOWA

One of the many stops made by Lewis and Clark during their exploration of the Missouri River in 1804-1805 was in the area now known as Council Bluffs. They, the first white men to stop here, held a meeting (or council) with the Otoe and Missouri Indians atop a high steep bluff.

Several historic occurrences happened in this town in the nineteenth century. The Mormons arrived here on January 14, 1846, after being driven out of Illinois. Before the year ended, they elected Brigham Young president of the Mormon Church, meeting in the newly built log tabernacle that seated a thousand worshipers.

In 1859, Abraham Lincoln, on one of his many speaking engagements as a private citizen, officiated here when this city was selected as the eastern terminus of the Union Pacific—the first transcontinental railroad to be built in the United States.

TREASURE ISLAND, FLORIDA

Spanish exploration of Florida's west coast began in the early 1500's. According to a local resident, a number of Spanish galleons, some with treasure, were sunk off the coast of this region.

 **13**

LIGHTHEARTED NAMES

There are many regional stories, fact and fancy, that describe local events, usually humorous, which eventually became names of towns. Such lighthearted names were adopted by down-to-earth folk who were blessed with the virtue of not taking themselves too seriously.

ALOHA, WASHINGTON

In the early 1900's two young men just out of college, W. H. Dole and Ralph Emerson, teamed up and founded this town. They set up a sawmill, later expanding their investment to a flour mill and then a large shingle mill.

Dole, a relative of the famous pineapple Doles, had been raised in Hawaii. He named the town Aloha after a Hawaiian word used for both greetings and good-byes.

TRUTH OR CONSEQUENCES, NEW MEXICO

In 1950 the people of Hot Springs, New Mexico, voted to change their town's name to Truth or Consequences. Ralph Edwards, MC of that radio program, had made an offer to give free national publicity to any town that would change its name to that of his program. True to his word, Edwards annually leads a group of stars to this New Mexico town to participate in the Truth or Consequences Fiesta. The people here thought so highly of Mr. Edwards that they named their main park in his honor.

One of the highlights of this vacation town is its famous thermal baths. For hundreds of years, different Indian tribes traveled to these hot springs, considered neutral territory, to bathe wounds suffered in battle. It was a favorite resting place for the Apache leader Geronimo.

OLD JOE, ARKANSAS

Old Joe got its name from a mountain located one thousand feet north of the town. It was previously called Naked Joe. The original name was submitted, but the postal service wouldn't go along with the naked part, so the town's residents compromised.

DELHI, LOUISIANA

The original name of this town was Deerfield because of the many deer that used to run in the nearby wooded area. The name was changed to Delhi, according to a senior town resident, Grandmother Tweedle, because of the following unusual occurrence:

> As I was on my way to school one morning, I saw a man ride up to a large oak tree, located about the place the First National Bank now occupies, and start to carve a name on the tree. On my way home from school that afternoon I saw that he had completed his work, and I read the name DELHI. This name was adopted by the people who were settling the little town, and so it has remained.

At the end of the Civil War Reconstruction years, the town became known as a hangout for Jesse and Frank James and their gang. According to local residents, the gang did not rob or harm them, conducting their thievery in Missouri and the central states. In fact, it is said, they were quite generous to the poor and needy in this region, the home of the James's relatives, Jace and Will.

ROMEOVILLE, ILLINOIS

The town was first named Romeo as a romantic mate for the city of Juliet, nine and half miles south. But in 1845 Juliet changed its name to Joliet in honor of Louis Jolliet, the French explorer and geographer, who once passed through the area. Sadly, Romeo residents responded by renaming their town Romeoville.

The town of Romeo, Colorado, has no Shakespearean roots. It was named after its original homesteader, a Mr. Romero. When he had applied for a post office, he was told that there already was a Romero in Colorado, so he dropped the second *r*.

OTHELLO, WASHINGTON

There is no connection between the name of this town and Shakespeare's play. In 1904, when a post office for this area was being established, a petition was sent to the people living within a ten-mile radius, asking them for possible names. Mrs. R. M. Chavis sent in "Othello," because it had been the name of a post office in Tennessee, where she had lived as a child.

CHICKEN, ALASKA

This region had an abundance of ptarmigans, which are birds that have plump bodies, strong feathered legs, and bright, reddish-brown plumage. Townspeople, writing to friends, had such a difficult time spelling the name that they started calling them chickens.

SAINT JO, TEXAS

This community, previously an important watering stop at the crossroads where the Chisholm Trail and the California Road met, was renamed for Joe Howell, who laid out the townsite. It is said that he opposed the sale of liquor in town, thus earning for himself, and the town, the name "Saint Jo."

WARSAW, NORTH CAROLINA

Thaddeus D. Love, conductor of the first train that ran through this community, took up residence here in 1838. His friends, familiar with the popular Jane Porter novel, *Thaddeus of Warsaw*, began calling him Thaddeus of Warsaw. Later, in 1855, the townspeople decided to incorporate their city with the name Warsaw.

IVANHOE, MINNESOTA

Ivanhoe, in Lincoln County, calls itself "The Story Book Town" because it was named after Sir Walter Scott's famous historical novel *Ivanhoe*.

At the turn of the last century, a representative of the Western Town Lot Company was reading the Scott novel while traveling by train to plot a new village. He was so impressed with the book that he not only called the new town Ivanhoe, but he used names from the book for its streets—Saxon, Rotherwood, Rowena, Division, George, Wallace, Rebecca, Huber, Sherwood, Norman, Harold, and Bruce.

HAMBURG, ARKANSAS

According to folklore, when this region was a crude settlement, surrounded by thick foliage, two itinerant hunters killed a pair of enormous deer. As they dressed their game, they were so astonished at the size of the animals' hams that they dubbed the settlement "Ham." It later became Hamburg.

SEVEN MILE, OHIO

Back in the days when the automobile was first developed, drivers used to stop and ask local residents how far the next big town, Hamilton, was. The farmers used to look slowly to the left and say: "Seven mile down the pike."

EMBARRASS, WISCONSIN

A century ago this northeastern part of Wisconsin was called the Pinery because of the vast pine forests, logging camps, and sawmills located there. Logs were sent to the mills in various ways: dragged along supply roads by oxen or horses, or put on logging sleighs and sent to the riverbanks, where they were floated to the sawmills in the spring. One of these rivers had so many snags and turns in it that it constantly jammed up the logs. This prompted the French-Canadian lumberjacks to refer to it as *Rivière Embarrassé—*"Tangled River." The village later took the name of the river, which English-speaking settlers called the Embarrass.

SMACKOVER, ARKANSAS

A group of French trappers and hunters from Louisiana settled here in 1844. Seeing that the area was covered with sumac shrubs, they referred to it as *sumac-couvert—*"sumac covered." Over the years American usage changed this to Smackover.

ENIGMA, GEORGIA

The reason why the people of this town chose the name Enigma, meaning "an inexplicable circumstance, event, or occurrence," is an enigma.

INDEX